APPLIED DESIGN
FOR PRINTERS

LECTOR HOUSE PUBLIC DOMAIN WORKS

APPLIED DESIGN FOR PRINTERS

HARRY LAWRENCE GAGE

ISBN: 978-93-5420-179-0

Published: 1920

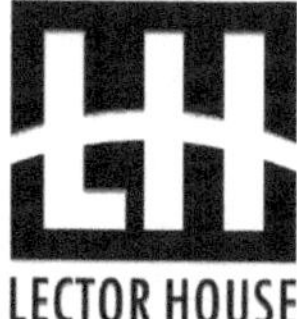

LECTOR HOUSE LLP
E-MAIL: lectorpublishing@gmail.com

TYPOGRAPHIC TECHNICAL SERIES FOR APPRENTICES—
PART VII. NO. 43

APPLIED DESIGN FOR PRINTERS

A HANDBOOK OF THE PRINCIPLES OF ARRANGEMENT, WITH BRIEF COMMENT ON THE PERIODS OF DESIGN WHICH HAVE MOST STRONGLY INFLUENCED PRINTING

BY

HARRY LAWRENCE GAGE

1920

FOREWORD

T HIS primer of design is an earnest effort to make intelligible to the apprentice student certain fundamental principles of arrangement and of ornamentation whose use is instinctive to the accomplished typographer.

It has been often written that there are no rules in Art, and equally often that the master artist (or craftsman) is he who can skillfully break all rules. It must be inevitable that the apprentice shall adhere too closely to each newly observed principle before his work can be a well-rounded embodiment of them all. To him is commended this exact procedure, recognizing, as his perception grows, that there are good reasons why traditions are emphasized here and all-embracing rules and formulae are not to be found.

Due credit must be paid to Mr. Ernest Allen Batchelder, who first devoted his pen and brush directly to the printer's problem in design, and who in turn gives honor to the influence of Mr. Denman Ross. Neither has expressed a method but has graphically analyzed the attitude of mankind during successive epochs toward those matters which deal with beauty.

It is to be hoped that this little book may serve as a simple guide and as a stimulant toward an extended study of the larger attributes of printing which are not concerned with utility alone. H. L. G.

CONTENTS

		Page
FOREWORD		v
• INTRODUCTORY		1
• THE SURFACE		3
• THE MATERIALS OF DESIGN		5
• THE QUALITIES OF DESIGN		7
• PROPORTION		13
• BALANCE.		18
• SYMMETRY.		22
• VARIETY		24
• MOTION		25
• ORNAMENT		28
• PERIODS OF DESIGN WHICH HAVE MOST AFFECTED PRINTING		36
• SUPPLEMENTARY READING		56
• REVIEW QUESTIONS		57
• GLOSSARY		60

APPLIED DESIGN FOR PRINTERS

INTRODUCTORY

R AW material may be made into a finished product which will have the quality of usefulness alone. Utility is the first purpose of most of the works of man. But when the maker is moved by pride in his work and a desire for beauty to make his handiwork pleasing in appearance as well as useful a second purpose is fulfilled. All civilization and most forms of savagery demand that the equipment of routine life shall be pleasing to the eye after its prime purpose of usefulness has been developed.

If an article be pleasing in appearance its making will have involved some of the elements of design. The relationship of its parts, the lines of its construction, its coloring, the manner in which it is ornamented will depend first upon its purpose, but will be guided by a group of recognized traditions which we call the *principles of design.*

Design governs the arrangement of masses, lines, and dots to secure the qualities of beauty and fitness.

Any piece of work which is definitely arranged with consideration for its various parts and their relationship is called, in the abstract, a "design." Thus we speak of a poster, a decorated wall, a building, or a printed page as "a design."

Any successful design will have the qualities of fitness and beauty. Fitness to purpose is largely a mechanical factor. An ugly building may protect its occupants from the weather, and an ugly printed page may be entirely legible. Beauty depends upon esthetic qualities; that is, upon the characteristics of the design which will appeal to the eye and mind through the consideration of—

Harmony (of shape, tone, color, and conception).

Balance and proportion (of mass, shape, and color).

Rhythm (of shape, line, tone, and color).

This conception of the elements of design covers all of the many things that mankind makes—buildings, or railroad trains, or sculpture, or paintings, or pottery, or furniture, or the printed page alike. In each, different though they be, the purpose of design is to relate the various surfaces, masses, and structural lines and to decorate or ornament the finished whole. Countless materials may be used and all the varied purposes of the equipment of mankind must be satisfied, but the application of the principles of design will be similar throughout. This point is emphasized so that the student of printing may find a common ground with the workers in all the fine and useful arts.

THE SURFACE

In the printed page, design is concerned with the arrangement of masses and lines on a flat surface—the face of the sheet of paper. Hence design in printing considers two dimensions only, width and length. The third dimension, depth, which must be treated in all but flat surfaces, can only be *represented* on the printed page and the means of showing depth is really an illusion by which the eye sees various colors and tones which convey a pictorial impression.

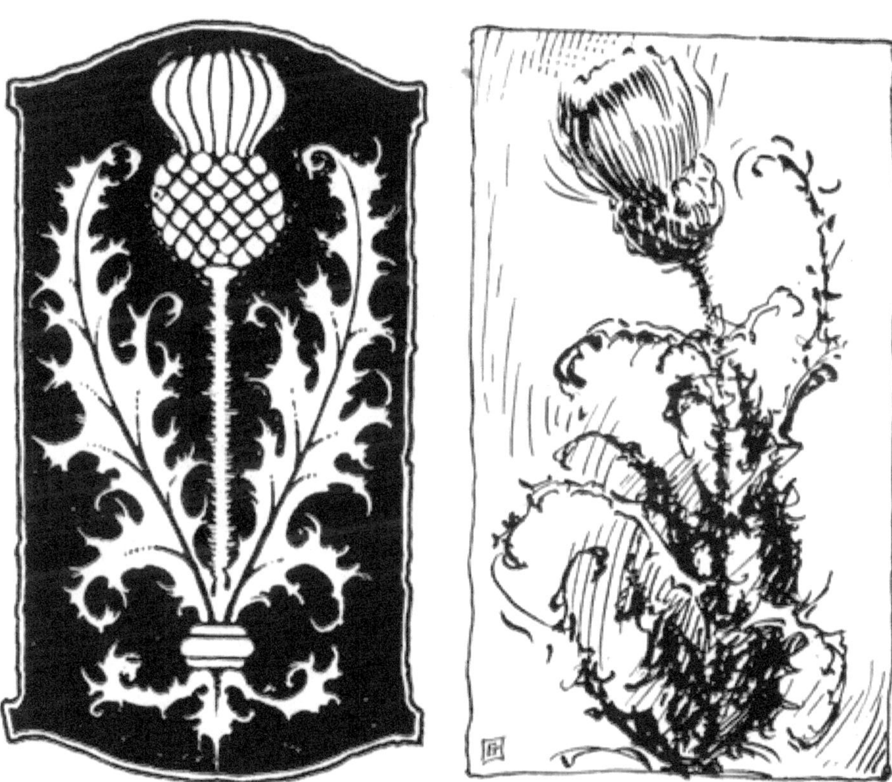

Fig. 1. A design of flat surfaces and a realistic pen sketch of the same subject.

It is important to note that *design* and *pictorial representation* serve each a different purpose in printing. Yet they are similar mechanically in that each requires a printing surface (type, borders, ornaments, and engravings) which may be prepared by the same mechanical procedures. The picture exists for its own interest or as an illustration for the text. As such it is merely an element in the design of the page. Decoration or ornament may be used to embellish the page, as a pattern on its flat surface, and may be related to the text, but need not serve as an illustration to it.

As an example: Much of the material devised for the decoration of the printed page (ornaments and borders) is derived from natural forms; i. e., leaves, flowers, etc. The leaves, stems, and flowers which are adapted to form the ornament shown in Fig. 1 are a flat pattern of black and white. The same material is rendered pictorially in the pen sketch accompanying the ornament. It will be observed that the flat treatment of the ornament depends upon arrangement of interesting flat masses for its significance. The pen sketch not only conveys an impression of the form of the natural objects, but it also suggests depth. A photograph of the natural objects, reproduced by a printing plate, would be still more realistic.

The preceding points have been given emphasis as a warning against a tendency to use pictures, however pleasing, as decorative material; or to allow design in printing to be concerned with a representation of depth. The same masses of shadow and light which express roundness or depth in a picture may be formed into decorative flat masses and thus embodied in the design of the page. In Fig. 2, A is a picture which might be used as an illustration or for its own interest. B is a flat rendering whose arrangement of masses suggests the pictorial interest of A without denying the flat surface upon which it is printed.

THE MATERIALS OF DESIGN

Since design is a matter of arrangement, its materials are the *masses, lines,* and *dots* which make up the whole form.

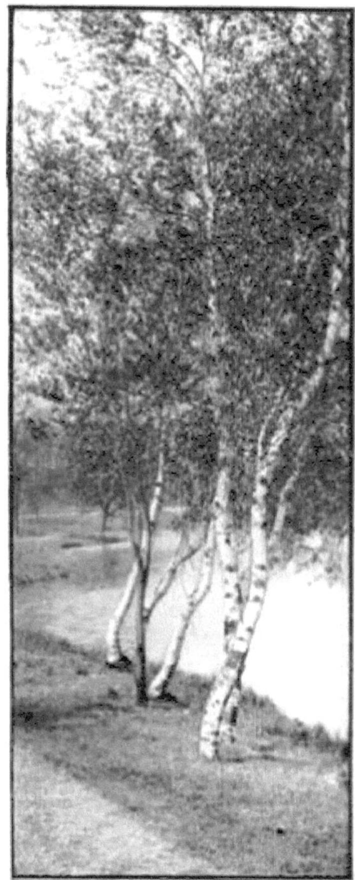

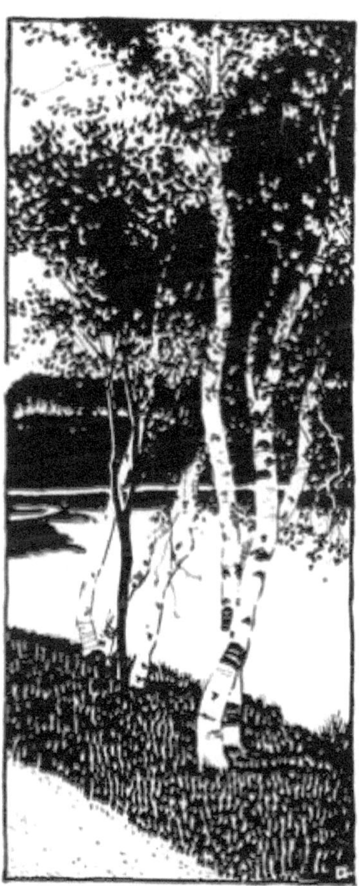

Fig. 2, A. Halftone engraving from a photograph, retaining full pictorial effect of depth, expressed in various gray tones and soft edges. This is an illustration.

Fig. 2, B. Decorative pen drawing from the same subject, telling the story of the photograph in flat surfaces of black and white. Suitable to decorate a type page.

A dot theoretically has no dimensions. And a line (being the path of a dot in motion) theoretically has length but no width. While if a line be moved sideways it produces a *mass* which has area and shape.

Practically, a dot may be larger than a pin point and may have definite shape—a square dot or a round dot. Also in the common terms of design a line may have width (often called weight). Thus we speak of a narrow or light line as contrasted with a wide or heavy line.

A mass will have shape, which is the impression conveyed to the eye by its general contour. It will have size or measure, which will be its actual or relative area. It will further have tone or color, its general relation in appearance to black and white or to the colors of the spectrum. Embodying these terms in an example: We may specify a mass square in shape, having an area of four square inches, and being gray in tone. These three characteristics, then, will identify and describe any mass.

In printing, the successive lines of type which form a paragraph, block, or connected series of paragraphs or blocks, are considered as a mass. An initial letter may be another mass; a head-band still another; and ornaments or illustrations may form other masses. All must be considered as mass elements in the design of the page, with rule borders as surrounding lines, or heavier designed borders as surrounding masses.

Thus all the component parts of the printed page are reduced to elements or materials of design, and with these materials an arrangement is to be made, for the sake of beauty, which will have the qualities of harmony, balance, proportion, and rhythm.

THE QUALITIES OF DESIGN

The dictionary defines *harmony*, in art, as "a normal state of completeness in the relation of things to each other." This "state of completeness" in a harmonious scheme is such that we have no desire to change or modify any detail or characteristic.

Balance is defined as "the state of being in equilibrium." In design this refers to the equilibrium or balance of attraction to the eye between the various masses.

Proportion is "the comparative relation of one thing to another" with respect to size.

Rhythm, in design, "is a movement characterized by regular recurrence of accent."

Let us discover the embodiment of these qualities of design with a simple experiment. Cut from black, dark gray, and light gray cover paper a miscellaneous assortment of small pieces as shown in Fig. 3. This group of squares, oblongs, triangles, diamonds, circles, and whatnot has none of the qualities of design as it appears in Fig. 3.

Choose from Fig. 3 certain pieces which seem to have a definite similarity of shape. Combine them with another rectangle, as in Fig. 4, and the result is certainly more orderly and pleasing than the unrelated tangle in Fig. 3. In Fig. 4 we have developed the quality of *shape harmony*.

But we note that in spite of the harmony of shapes in Fig. 4 some of the pieces of paper seem unduly prominent because of their blackness. They do not seem harmonious with the gray tone of the others. If we replace them with other pieces gray in color, as in Fig. 5, the result will be a more pleasing relationship of tone throughout the design. Thus we have made a simple demonstration of *tone harmony*.

If our pieces of paper were of various colors we could make another arrangement to express a *color harmony*. The problem of color, however, has so many phases that it is considered separately in this series.

If rhythm is to give us a "regular recurrence" of various features of a design, it will be possible to choose a combination of pieces of paper which will show a rhythmic arrangement, Fig. 6. It will be noticeable here that the shapes occur in successive groups which repeat an idea.

We may also arrange a series of pieces in which the tones are rhythmic, progressing from light to dark in repeated groups. This will be a simple example of *tone rhythm*, Fig. 7.

Summing up the experiment thus far the following definitions may be noted:

Shape harmony will exist when masses similar in contour or shape are used to form a design.

Tone harmony results from the use of tones in a design which carry a feeling of relationship.

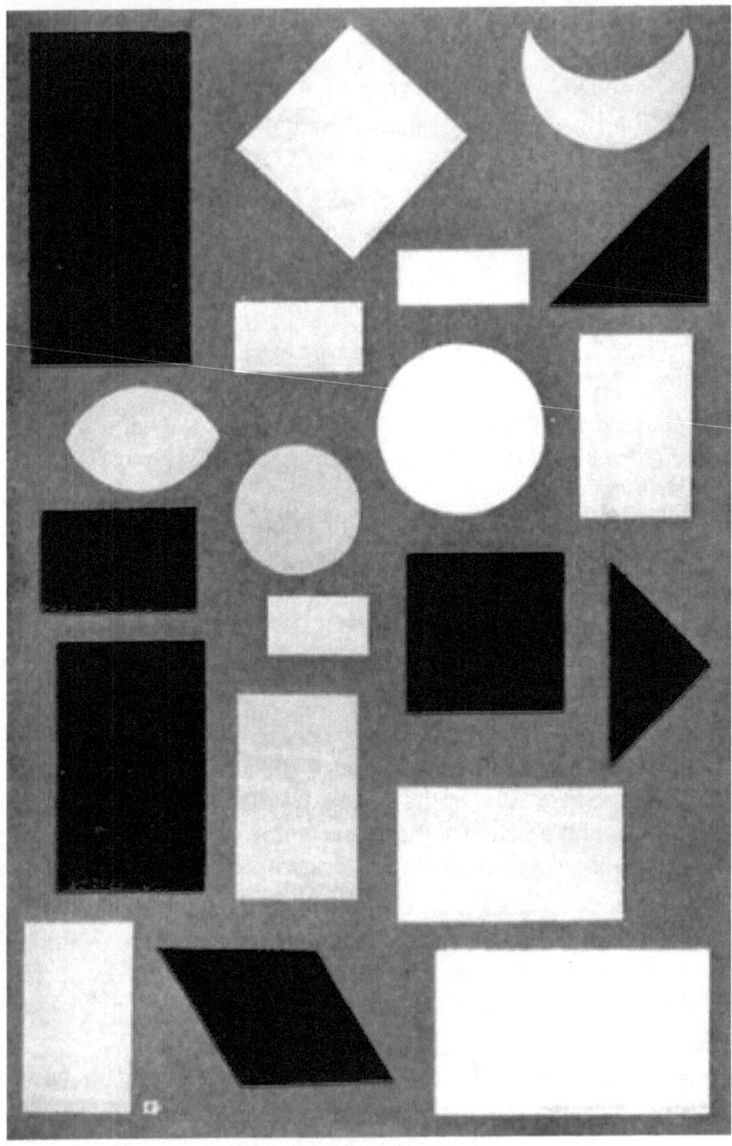

Fig. 3. A group of miscellaneous masses having various measures, shapes, and tones. Arranged without thought of design.

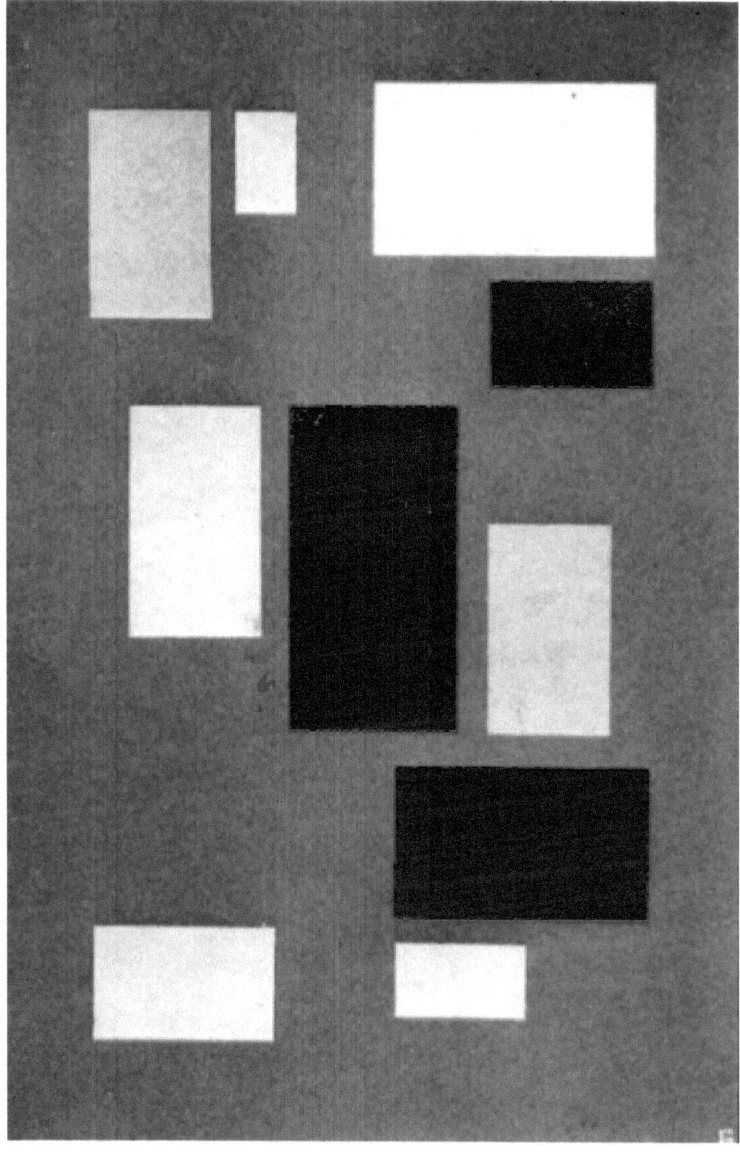

Fig. 4. Units selected from Fig. 3, having a common similarity of shape. But they are not harmoniously related in tone.

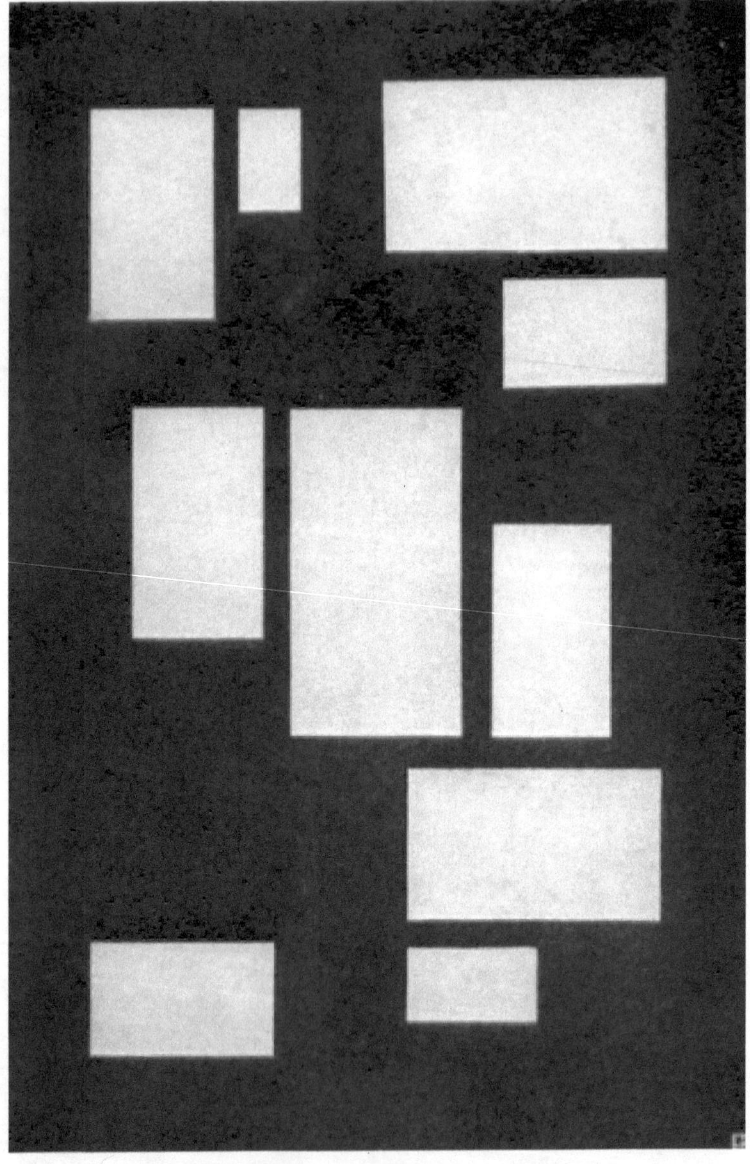

Fig. 5. The same shapes used in Fig. 4, substituting equal tones of gray as need-
ed to produce harmony throughout.

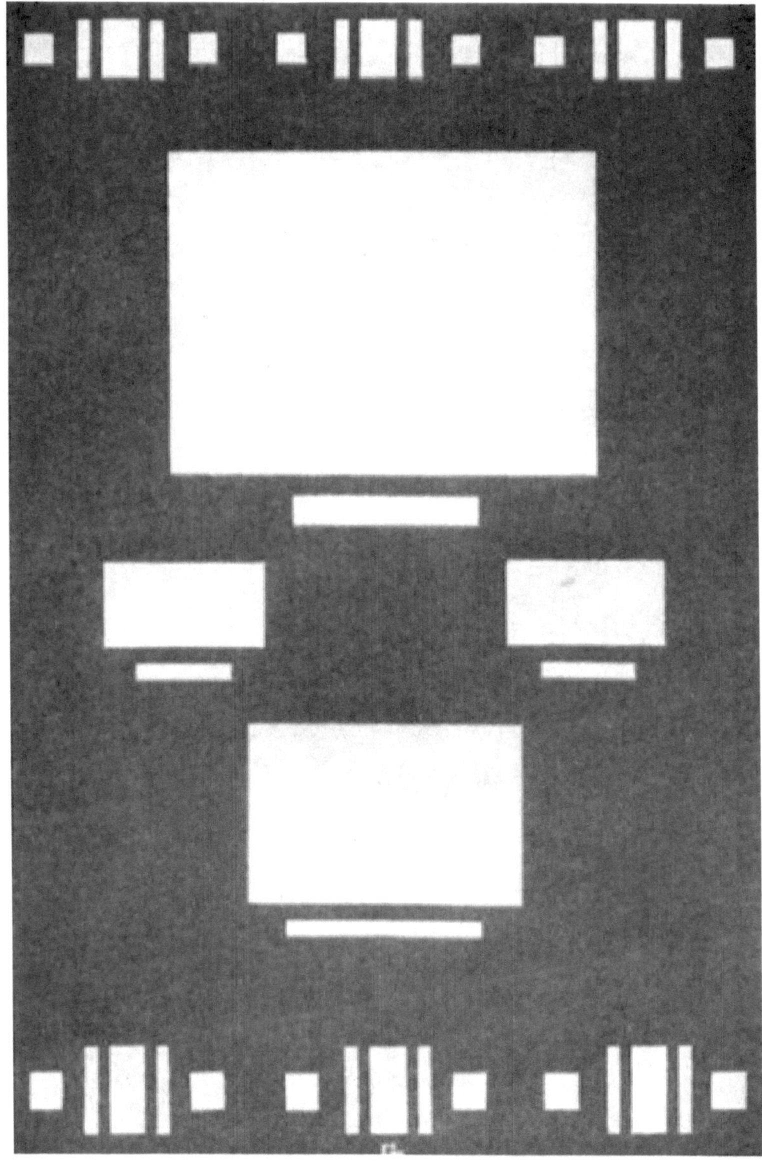

Fig. 6. Simple development of shape and measure rhythm such as might occur on a printed page. Masses should be related in measure as well as in shape.

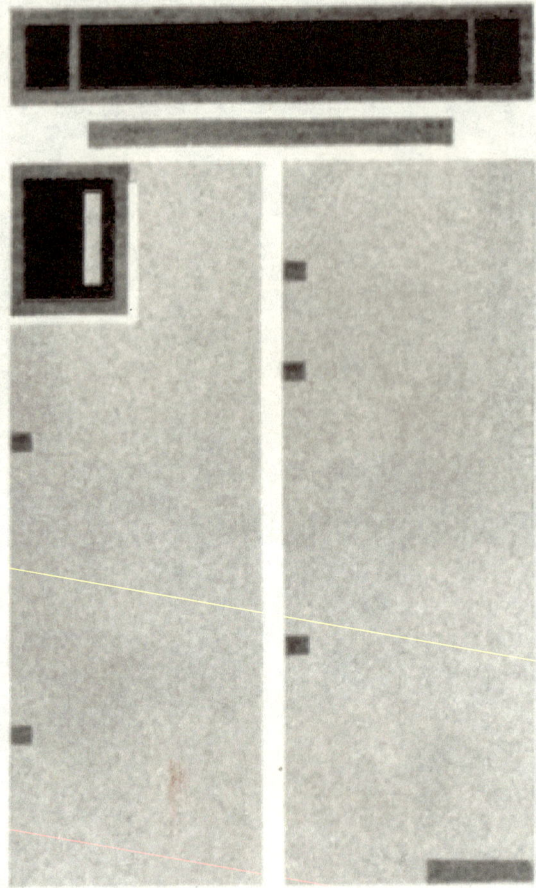

Fig. 7. Simple illustration of tone rhythm as it may occur on a type page. The tones progress from the white of the margins through the light gray masses of type, to the darker grays of decorations.

Shape rhythm is the regular recurrence of similar shapes in a design or a rhythmic increase or decrease in the size of shapes used in a design.

Tone rhythm is a recurrence of similar tones or a regular progression of related tones from light to dark or the reverse through a design.

The four qualities above are so closely related that there is often no definite dividing line between them; indeed, a successful design will embody them all.

PROPORTION

Our definition of proportion as a comparative relationship of size is so broad that any sizes may be in proportion. The quality of proportion in design is always assumed to be a *pleasing* relationship of sizes. It thus becomes necessary to determine what relationship of sizes will be most pleasing.

The use of equal masses in a design is monotonous. The eye finds variety of size more interesting. But to determine what form of variety is most interesting we must find, if possible, the ideal area relationship between masses in a design. This problem has of necessity been solved by the designers of all nations and all periods, and it is interesting to note that the result has everywhere been practically the same.

Let us arrive at the expression of good proportion by the simple means of dividing a rectangle into two parts which will have the most interesting relationship. This rectangle is A in Fig. 8. B shows a division into equal parts, the result being uninteresting and monotonous. In C the division gives a feeling that the lower part is too large; it is crowding the upper and the result is not pleasing. The relationship in D is so nearly equal that the division seems to have been an inaccurate effort to locate the center. Somewhere between the division point in C and that in D will probably be the best point. Repeated trials will locate the point about as in E, which will be found to lie about two-fifths of the distance down from the top. This will give the upper area in E an area of 2 and the lower an area of 3. Hence the relationship or proportion is said to be as 2 is to 3. By the term "good proportion," or merely the word "proportion," in speaking of design this ratio of 2 to 3 is assumed.

It is interesting to note that when a space has been divided into the ratio of 2 to 3, the relationship of the smaller to the larger is practically the same as the relationship of the larger to the original whole. Or, mathematically, if the original, having an area of 5, is divided into parts of 2 and 3, then 2 is to 3 as 3 is to 5, — a ratio which is approximately true.

The student of architecture finds the most careful consideration of proportion in the relationship of spaces throughout all the architectural orders. In printing, the designer must be guided by the same traditions.

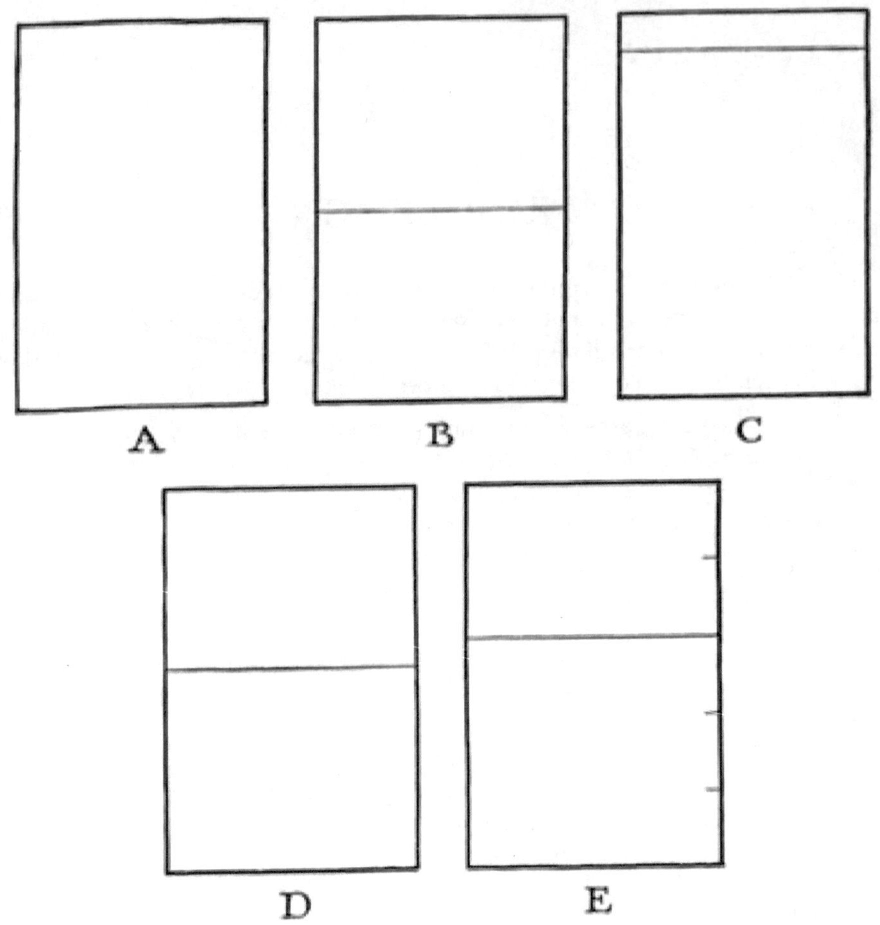

Fig. 8. The division of a rectangle, A, to secure spaces of interesting relationship. Equal division in B. Overbalanced effect in C. Too nearly equal in D.
More interesting in E, where the relationship of spaces is as 2 is to 3.

The most simple application of proportion to the division of a printed page
occurs when a single type line or compact group of lines is to be placed on the
page (Fig. 9).

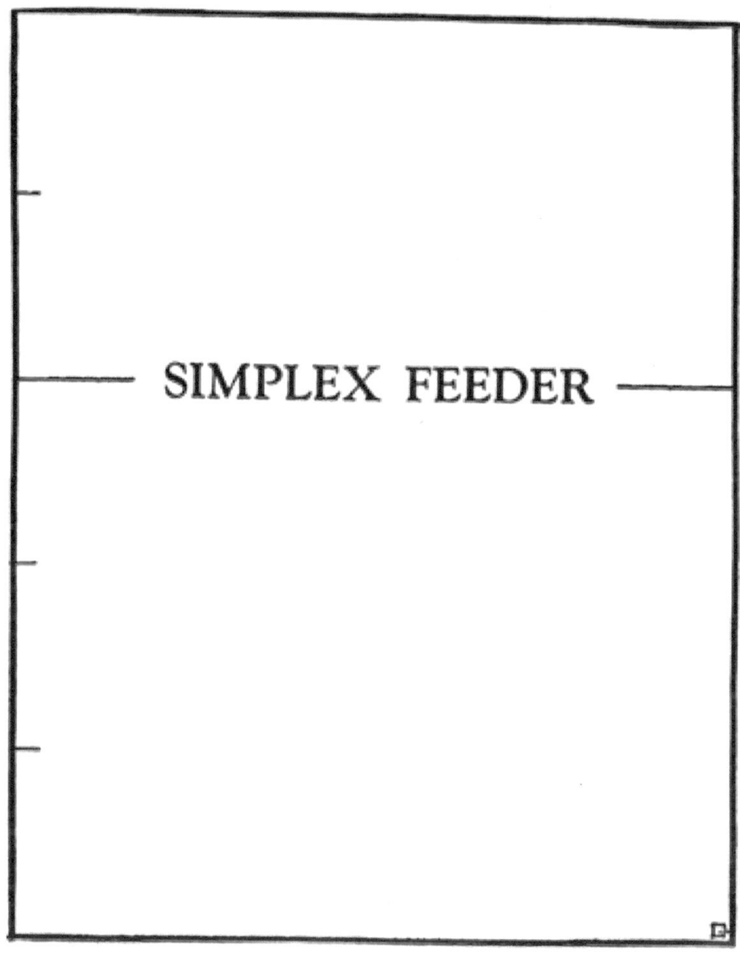

Fig. 9. "Spotting" a single line on a page so that it makes an interesting division of space. There are 2 parts of white space above and 3 parts below.

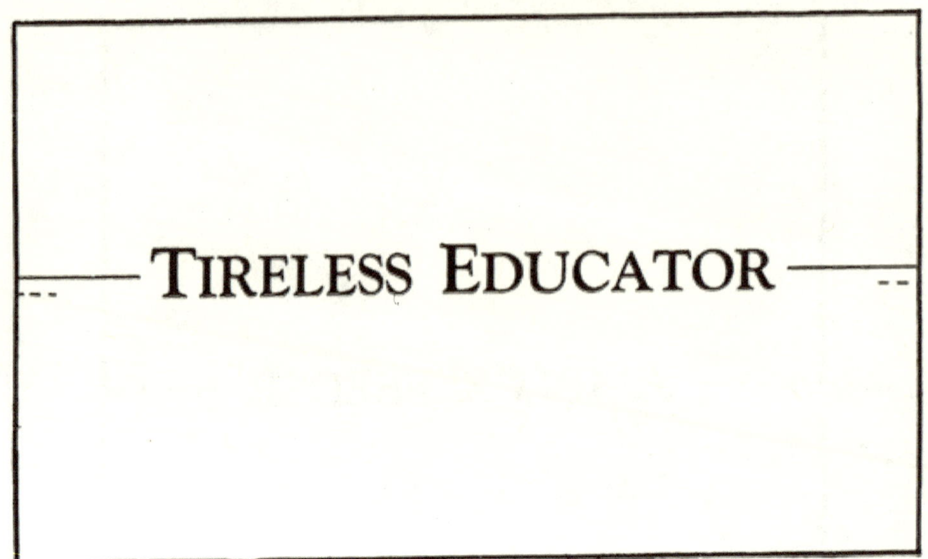

Fig. 10. Placing a single line so that it will appear to be centered. The dotted lines show the mathematical center of the vertical side. The straight lines show the center of the type line.

It is unfortunate that it is so easy to divide space mechanically in a type page by using identical measures of furniture or slugs above and below. When, in certain instances (as in a business card), tradition demands that a line be "centered" vertically, it will be found that the exact centering of the line will make it appear a bit low. An optical illusion demands that such a line be raised slightly if it is to appear in the vertical center (Fig. 10). This apparent center is called "the optical center."

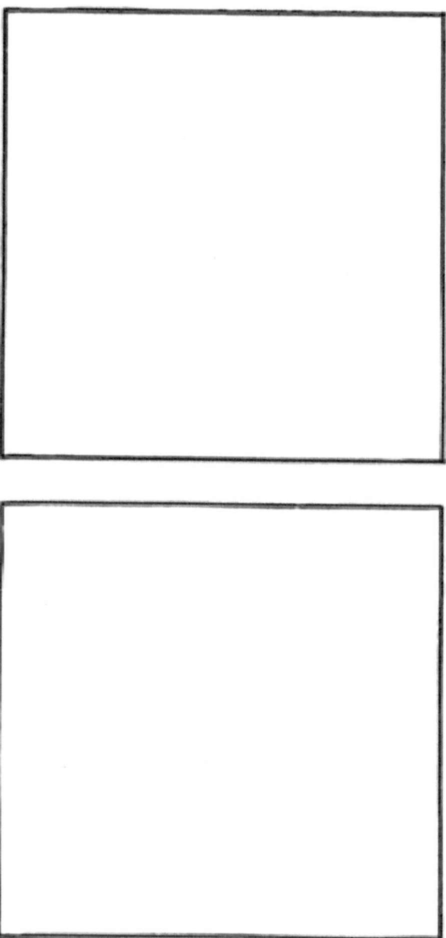

Fig. 11. A true square above and an optically corrected square below. Psychologists explain that the eyes find it more difficult to judge the length of vertical lines, hence are inclined to exaggerate them.

The same condition makes it necessary when an apparent square is to be used that the width of the "square" be slightly greater than the height. (Fig. 11.)

BALANCE

The physical equilibrium which exists in the balanced "seesaw" of our childhood and the optical balance which is the result of the proper adjustment of masses within the confining edges of a design are similar, in that each is an equalizing of forces of attraction. In the former the force is gravity; in the latter, the attraction to the eye, which varies with the size and tone of the mass. While the force of gravity usually brings balancing masses to a horizontal alignment, optical balance may bring the masses in a design into equilibrium on any desired line, horizontal, vertical, or diagonal.

The attraction which a mass possesses varies directly with its size and tone. Thus a mass of four square inches, solid black, will be twice as strong in attraction value as a mass of two square inches, solid black. It will also be twice as strong in attraction value as a mass of four square inches, neutral gray (the gray being half the value of black). The attraction value of gray tones particularly affects the consideration of blocks of type which vary in depth of tone according to the blackness of the type face, closeness of spacing, etc.

Since the "seesaw" must have its sawhorse and the weighing scale its point of support, it follows that any condition of equilibrium, physical or optical, demands a point of balance. In design, this point will determine the location of the related masses. It will be apparent upon further thought that the point of balance should have some relationship to the edge or confines of the design.

The confining edge of the design is usually a rectangle, on the printed page. The location of a point of balance within this rectangle tends to divide it. How shall it be divided in the most interesting way? By applying the ratio of good proportion. So the point of balance may be located usually on a line which divides the page into parts of 2 and 3.

When equal masses are to be balanced it is obvious that they will be equidistant from the point of balance. (Fig. 12.)

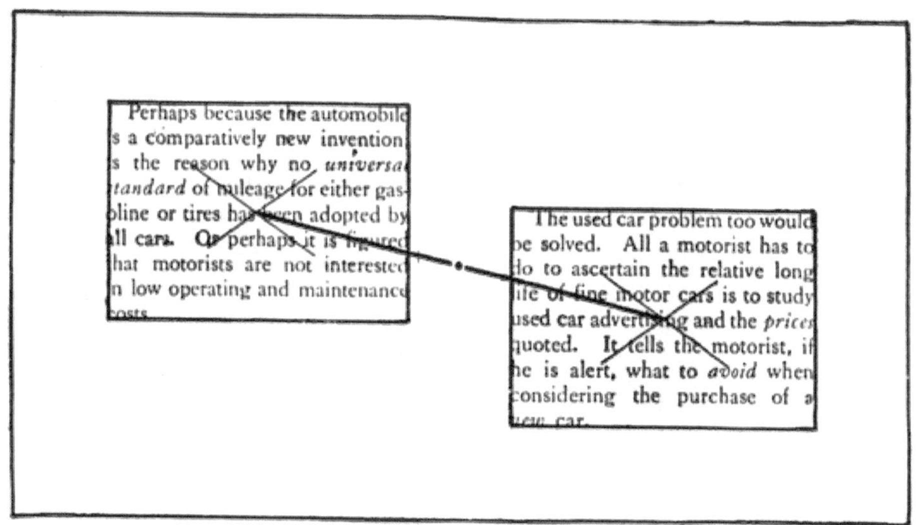

Fig. 12. Equal masses balanced at equal distance from the center point.

When the masses are unequal the point is at unequal distances from the centers of the masses. These unequal distances have the same ratio as the masses themselves, but the larger mass is always the shorter distance from the point. If 1 pound is to balance 4 pounds it is obvious that the 1-pound mass must be 4 times as far from the point of balance as the 4-pound mass.

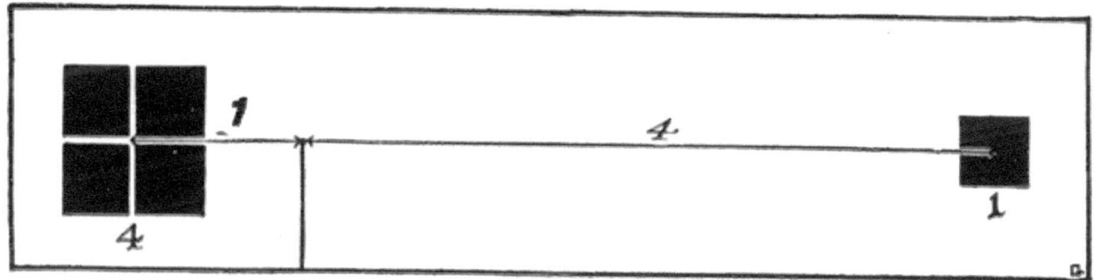

Fig. 13. Mass of 4 units balanced by 1 unit.

Hence, to balance two masses in a rectangle, the point of balance will be found by proportion, placing it on a line which divides the rectangle into parts of 2 to 3. The balancing of the masses across this point will then be a matter of determining their relative distances from it. It is apparent that the larger of two masses may be far enough from the point of balance so that it will force the smaller entirely out of the rectangle. It is of course easy to move the larger closer to the point which automatically brings in the smaller. What constitutes a proper distance from the edge of the rectangle will be discussed under "Margins," in the book on Typographical Design.

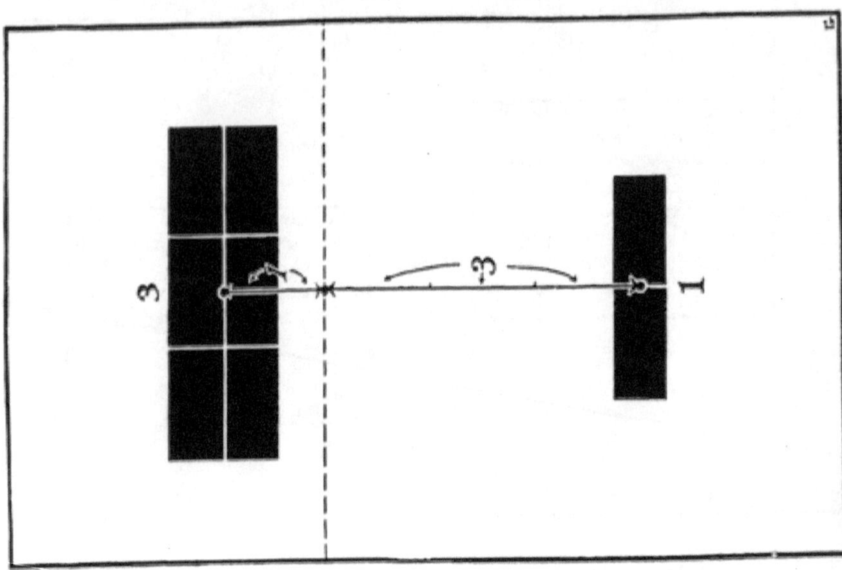

Fig. 14. Mass of 3 units balanced by mass of 1 unit, taking the point of balance
upon the line which divides the space in good proportion.

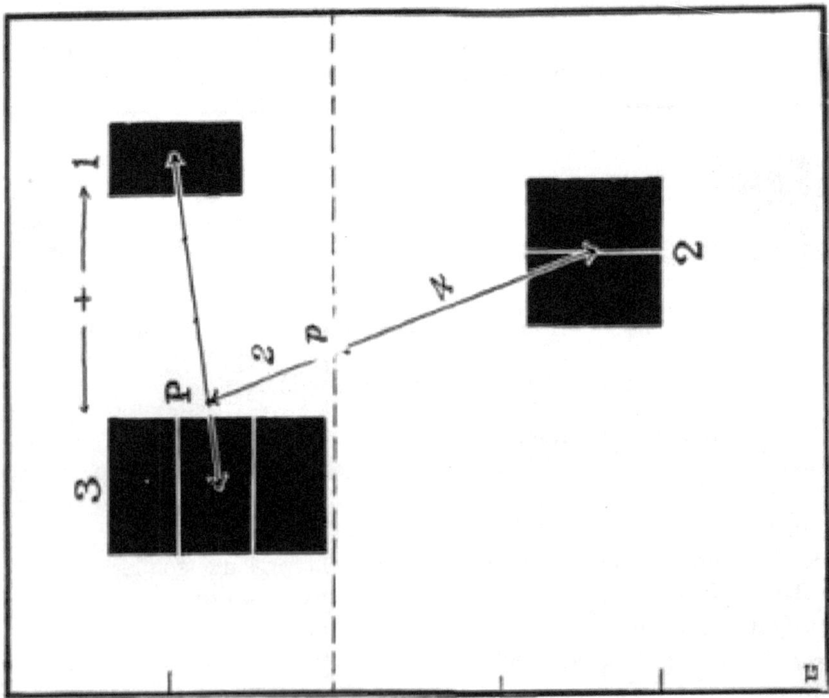

Fig. 15. Measures of 3 and 1 balanced by a measure of 2, the point of balance
dividing the space in good proportion.

The balance of three or more masses within a rectangle involves the consideration of two at a time, balancing the pair or pairs with the remaining mass or masses.

In Fig. 15, masses 1, 2 and 3 are to be balanced within the rectangle. Balancing 3 with 1 gives the balancing point P. Taking 3 plus 1 from the point P, we locate the mass 2 to balance them across the line AB which divides the rectangle in good proportion. The point p then becomes the balancing point for the entire group. Mathematically, 3 plus 1 equal 4; 4 is twice 2; therefore the mass 2 must be twice as far from the point p as the balanced masses 3 plus 1.

Two other combinations might have been worked out with the masses in Fig. 15: 3 plus 2, balanced by 1, the mass 1 being placed five times as far from the point p as would the point P. Or 2 plus 1 might have been balanced by 3, in which case the distances would have been equal.

The application of these principles of balance to the problems of typography is largely a matter of influence. The typographer should be guided by them but he need not make mathematical calculations if his eyes be trained to judge relative attraction values so that he can arrange his various masses to secure balance.

SYMMETRY

When two parts of a design are equal in every respect so that if the design were folded over one-half would superimpose in every detail with the other half, then a state of *symmetry* exists and the design is said to be *symmetrical*. The line upon which such a design would be folded, or, in other words, the line which bisects a symmetrical design, is called its *axis*.

The printed page is often symmetrical with respect to its vertical axis (Fig. 16).

In Fig. 16 the line AB is the vertical axis of the page.

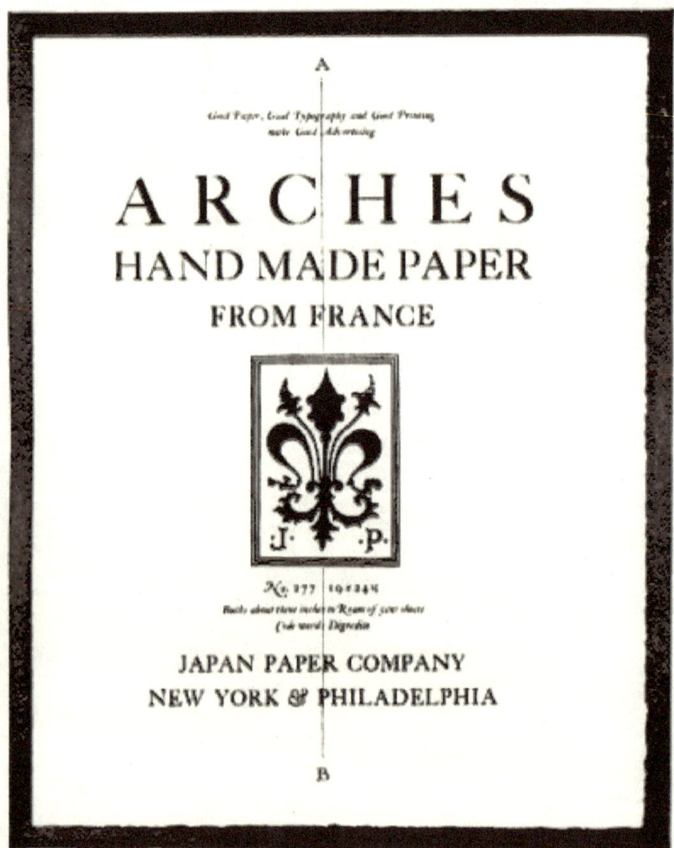

Fig. 16. Type page, symmetrical with respect to its vertical axis.

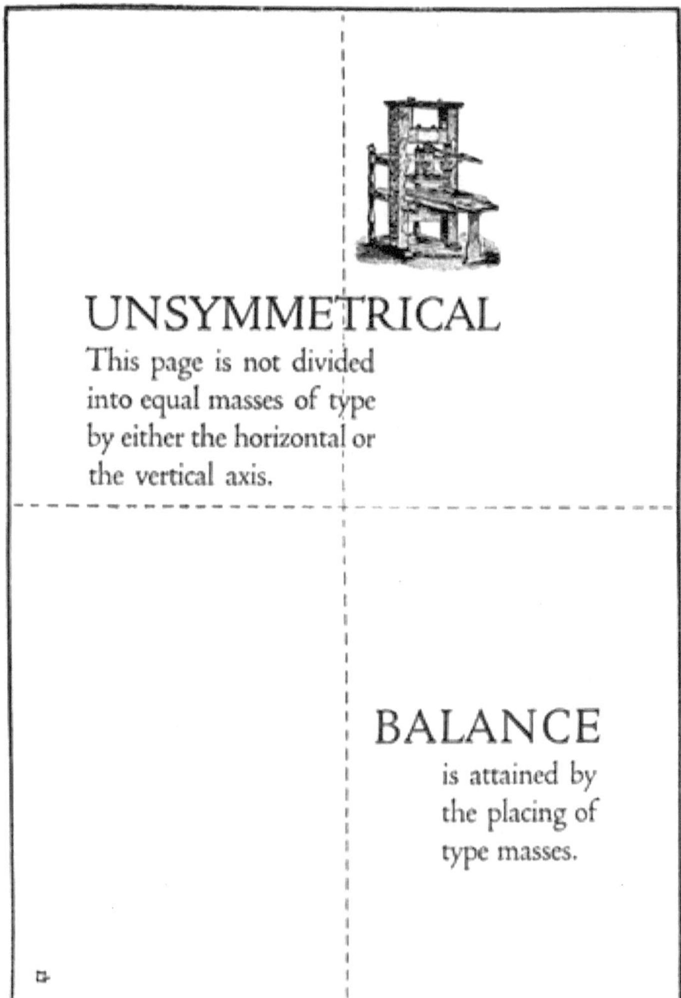

Fig. 17. Page arranged for variety. Not symmetrical on either axis. This arrangement is frequently used in advertising display, but is rare in book work.

It is rarely possible that the printed page can be symmetrical with respect to its horizontal axis. Such a state would involve a division of the page below its optical center and would also have an uninteresting division of its spaces, with equal masses above and below. It should be noted that symmetry on the vertical axis permits full variety in the size of the masses used.

VARIETY

The absence of symmetry in a design gives it the character of *variety*, which may be defined as a state of inequality in the arrangement of the parts of a design.

In Fig. 17, neither the horizontal axis nor the vertical axis divides the page so that its units are symmetrically arranged.

MOTION

In any arrangement, pictorial or decorative, the eye of the observer is attracted to various parts in succession, depending on their character and position with respect to each other. This quality, called motion, will be more pronounced as the several units tend to lead more definitely from one to another. Fig. 18 shows the path which the eye follows as it looks at the ornament. In pictorial composition the same quality is employed to emphasize the story to be told or the character of the arrangement used by the painter. Then it is called "line." This quality of design is not to be confused with "action," which is the depiction of a figure in motion, as shown in Fig. 19.

Fig. 18. The diagram shows the motion of the eye as it perceives the design above. This motion is due to line entirely, not to accents of tone.

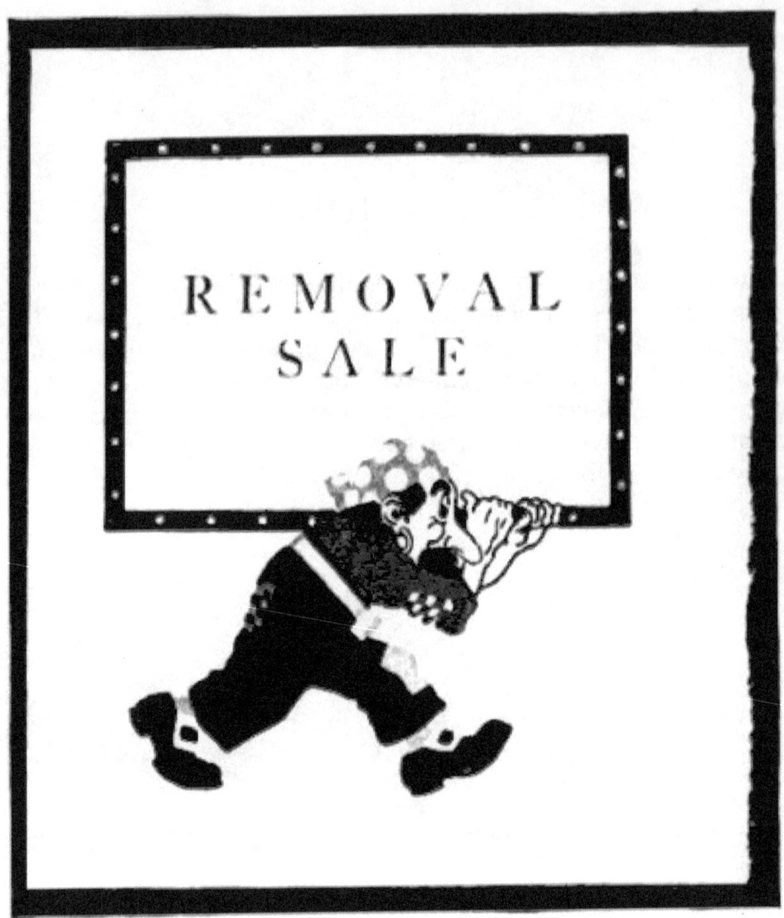

Fig. 19. Showing action in the figure depicted, without motion in design.

On the printed page the eye may be definitely directed from one unit to another through this quality of motion, which forms a very valuable resource for the printer. Fig. 20 is a diagram of a simple use of motion, the eye progressing as indicated by the arrows through the masses which make up the page.

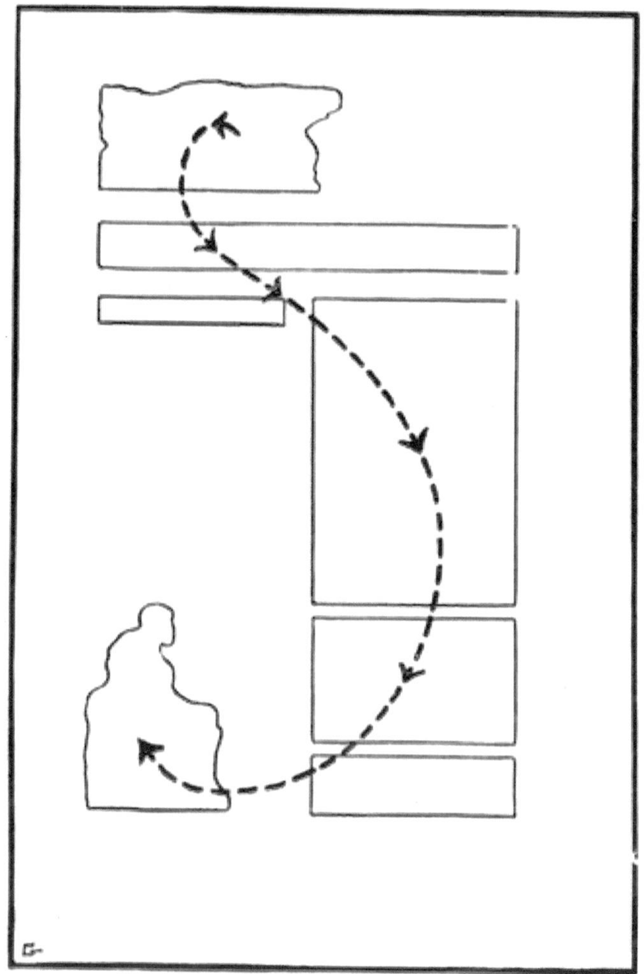

Fig. 20. Diagram of motion as employed in advertising to lead the eye progressively through a page.

ORNAMENT

While the elements of design concern all the parts of a proposed scheme (on the printed page, its masses of type, decorative border, head-band, initial letters, tail-piece, etc.) certain parts will be used solely to beautify the whole design. They ornament or decorate it. "Ornament is a means by which Beauty or Significance is imparted to Utility."

Ornament may be either Symbolic or Esthetic.

Symbolic ornament consists of elements or forms chosen because they are significant of the purpose of the design.

In Fig. 22, the ornament is symbolic in its close connection with the message conveyed by the type.

Esthetic ornament consists of forms chosen for their beauty alone. In Fig. 23, the head-band and initial are pleasing in design and they beautify the page without having the slightest relation to the text of the page.

Esthetic ornament characterizes the periods of design which have had the most important influence in the development of printing: the Greek, Roman, and Renaissance.

Symbolic ornament is found in Egyptian, Assyrian, Byzantine, Scandinavian, Celtic, Persian, Indian, Gothic, Chinese, and Japanese design. For intimate study of these various styles and periods the reader is referred to the various books listed in the bibliography.

Fig. 21. Ornament designed with natural forms.

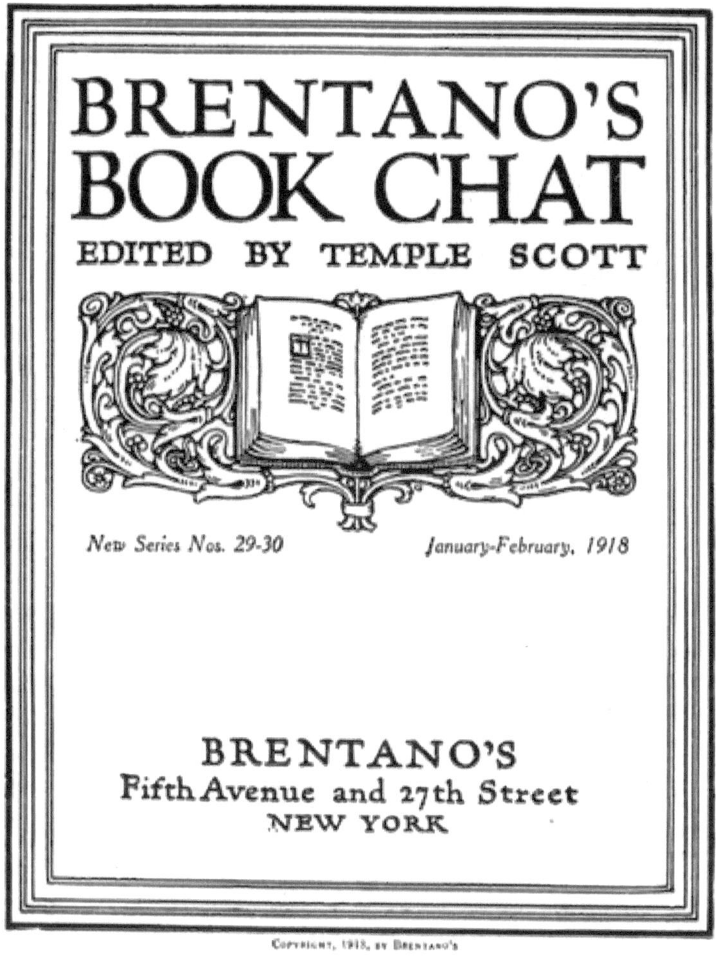

Fig. 22. House-organ cover design by Mr. F. W. Goudy, in which the ornament
is symbolic of the message of the page.

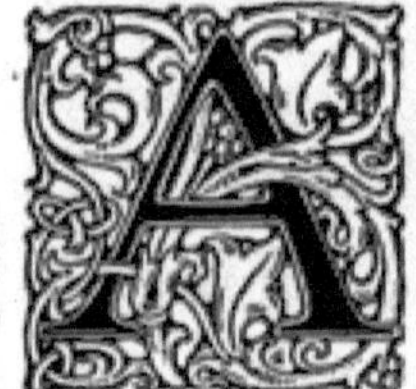

TRUE PRINTER CRAFTSMAN is never a mere manufacturer of printing. He is first the psychologist in the development of his product; he is the artist in the judgment and application of his materials; the artisan in the manipulation of his types and machines; the scientist in his solution of technical problems; the accountant in his records of income and outgo; the engineer in the maintenance of production and the executive control of his business. ¶ A young man may make a printer of himself without this multiplex personality but he will not be among the men who are to restore the Graphic Arts to their rightful position among the professions. If he happily possesses an instinct for the fundamentals of the printing trade, sometimes he may be guided further to acquire the principles of art, science, and the management of business. ¶ To lead coming generations of printers toward the ideals of master craftsmanship is the highest purpose of a technical school of printing, whose studies must be pursued not alone in the shop but also in the environment of the art school and the scientific school. These are the vital conditions under which the potential master printers of the future are being developed in the Department of Printing, Carnegie Institute of Technology, Schenley Park, Pittsburgh, Pennsylvania.

Fig. 23. Type page decorated with esthetic ornament. Much of the decorative material available to printers is of this character. Since the printer need not study its symbolic significance he may choose such decoration for its qualities of tone and good drawing.

Ornament may be natural or inventive. Natural ornament confines itself to the rendition in decorative design of forms chosen from nature, either animate of inanimate. Inventive ornament consists of elements not derived from any natural source. It is usually geometric in character; that is, it is rendered in patterns and masses expressed in geometric shapes.

A SINGLE DECORATIVE SPOT OF GEOMETRIC ORNAMENT

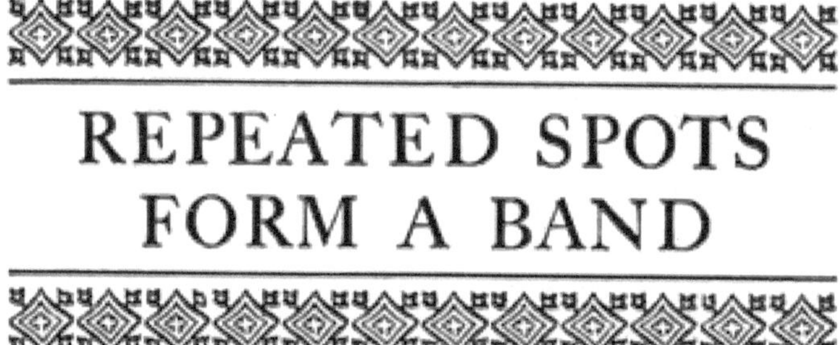

REPEATED SPOTS FORM A BAND

Fig. 24. Type border used as geometric ornaments.

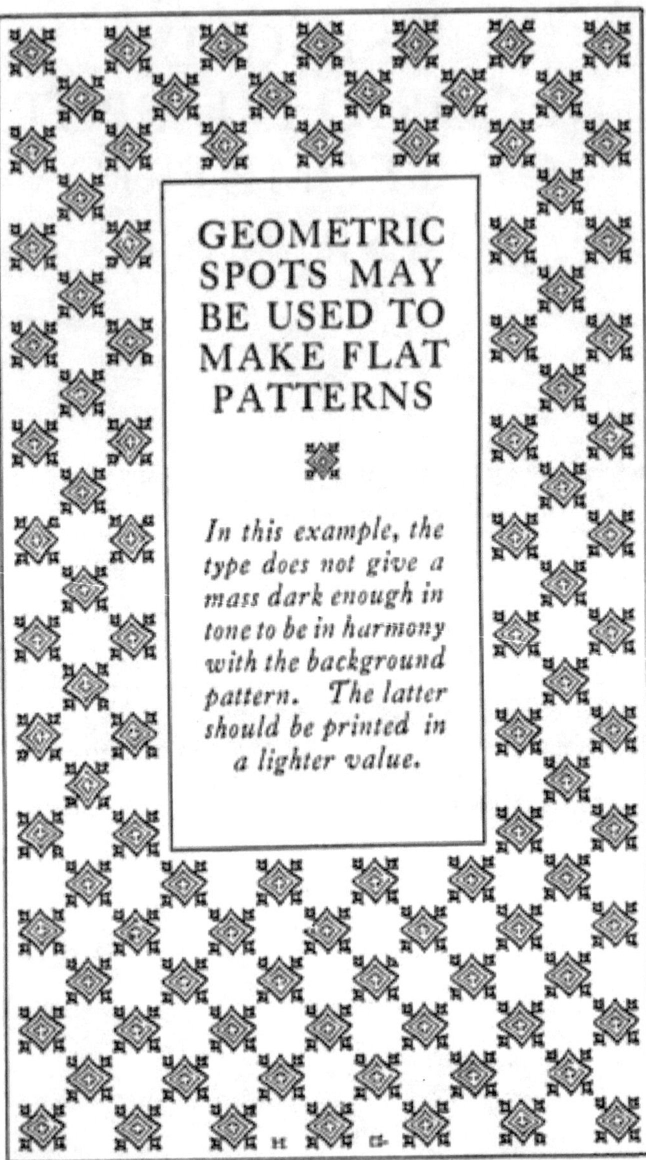

Fig. 25. Further use of type border to make a flat pattern or "all-over" design. Compare the effect with that shown in the facing illustration.

In the artistic development of the various races, geometric design has often been the result of religious restrictions upon the imitation of any animate forms. The Mahometans have developed it to its highest type of expression. Arabian and Moorish architecture and handicrafts are the best examples, with the crystal beauty of the Alhambra, the wonderful palace built by the Moors in Spain, as the supreme achievement of geometric design.

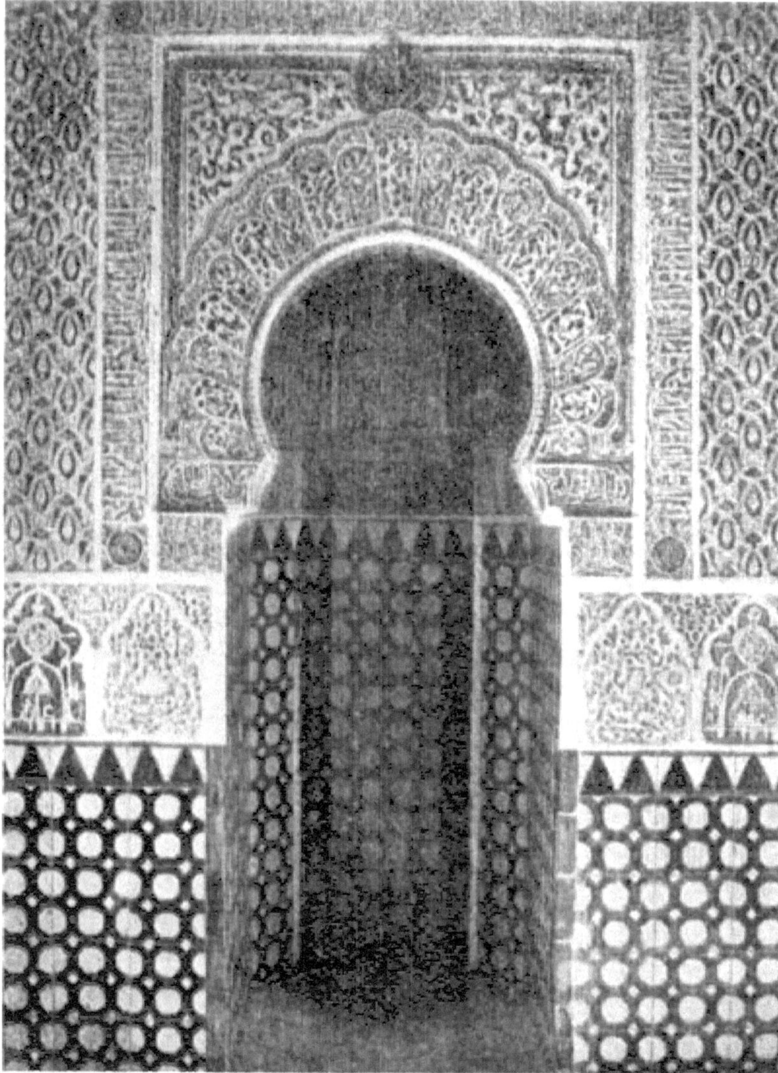

Fig. 26. A niche in the Alhambra, at Granada, Spain. Showing characteristic Moorish ornamentation.

Geometrical design uses simple materials, being the oldest of the elements of decoration. The implements of savages and the tattooing of the Indians prove this. From the first crude expressions of the original squares, circles, zigzag lines, and sundry simple combinations, gradual development led finally to the delicate forms of Moorish design. The elaboration of this style involves deep mathematical problems and careful draftsmanship.

The majority of geometrical ornaments may be divided into three groups. As we find them in typographical material these groups are bands or borders, made up visually of repeated units or spots; enclosed spaces or panels; and unlimited flat patterns or "all-over" designs.

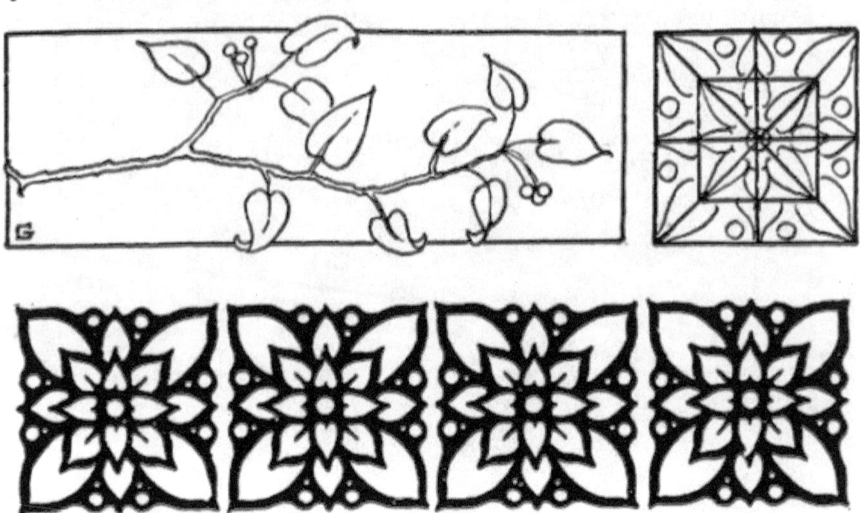

Fig. 27. The development of a motif (stems, leaves, and berries) into a decorative spot. Diagram in the upper corner shows the geometrical arrangement of the material. The spot has been repeated to form a band.

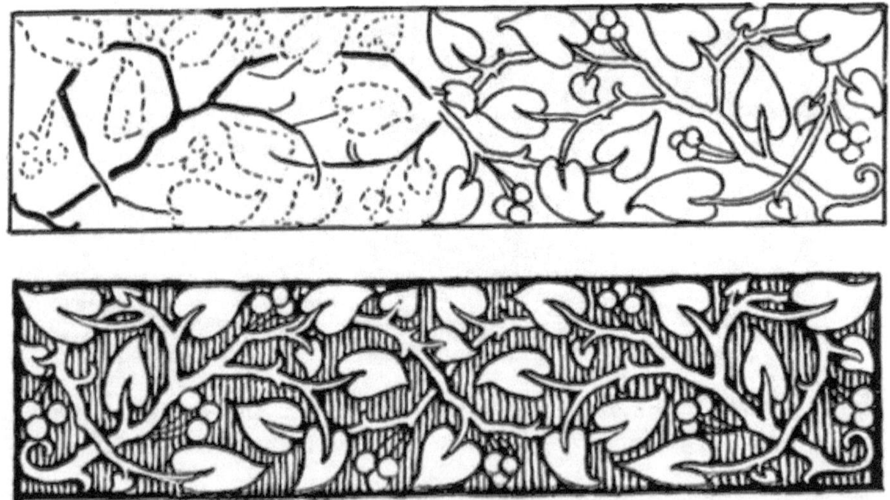

Fig. 28. Development of the motif used in Fig. 27 into a natural ornament. The forms and growth are not distorted but the rendering is in flat surfaces to hold the decorative quality.

In nearly every style and period of design the plant-world has been the biggest source of material for adaptation. The direct imitation of natural forms, keeping as much as possible of their shape, color, formation, etc., is called naturalistic design.

A departure from the exact details of the natural form, forming the design according to the rules of rhythm and symmetry, with strict attention to regularity leads to a result more artificial in character.

Whether the ornament you consider be naturalistic or artificial, the original source, which is the plant-form or other natural form from which the design was made, is called the *motif* of the design. It is interesting to survey the world about you and note here and there a recognizable motif in the design of wallpaper, hangings, furniture, rugs, books, and so on all through the works of man.

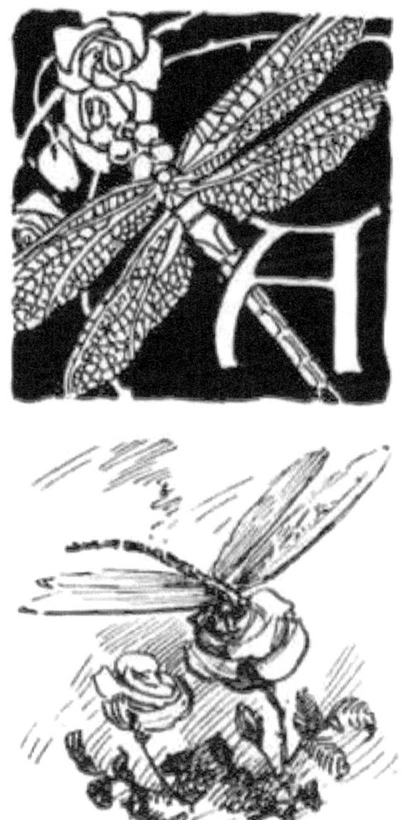

Fig. 29. Initial letter decorated with natural ornament and a pen sketch treating the motif in a more realistic way. Further emphasis of the essential flatness of surface in material that is to decorate a flat sheet of paper.

The development of a motif into ornament or decoration calls for the use of all the principles thus far established, plus familiarity with the medium to be used and the inventiveness that comes only with some experience. If the reader lacks this experience and is interested in undertaking to devise ornament or decoration with pen, pencil, or brush, he is advised to consult some one or more of the books on the subject which are listed in the bibliography. If he has facility with his pencil and enthusiasm for the work he will find it a most fascinating undertaking.

PERIODS OF DESIGN WHICH HAVE MOST AFFECTED PRINTING

The student of design finds that historical study of his subject carries him through the entire history of art, from the crude expressions of prehistoric man down the long and varied centuries to the styles and fancies of the present day. He will find his theme closely interwoven with the story of the development of races, the rise and fall of nations, the whole thrilling drama of ancient and modern history.

Printing, as a means of making records and of embodying and illustrating thought, has given us the wide field of literature on design. But in the making of books as an application of design, and in the making of all other forms of printed matter, printers since Gutenberg have been influenced by relatively few of the many distinct periods through which art has come. And those few have usually been the artistic feeling which prevailed at the time the printers lived.

To trace the periods of design that have most influenced printing is to tell in part the history of the craft. Since that subject is developed elsewhere in this series, suffice it to follow briefly the steps through which the making of books has passed.

Since the invention of movable types came opportunely to meet the desire for enlightenment by means of books, it was natural that printed books should be planned closely to imitate the hand-written or lettered books. These latter, having been produced for centuries by the men of the church to whom had been given training in the arts, had been brought to a high state of perfection in design. It has often been said that Gutenberg's forty-two line Bible, one of the first books printed from type, has never been surpassed in pure beauty of design and in the rich quality of its type masses.

But the first books printed from type were all of religious character, and the type itself was designed to imitate the black, condensed "text" letter forms which had been developed by the scribes. The elaborate initial letters which marked the sundry divisions of thought were repeated by the early printers, sometimes to be illumined by hand and later as engravings on wood or metal. There was no distinct departure from the ecclesiastical style of the monks save as was necessitated by the mechanical limitations of the new process of printing. Hence came a style which marked the first years of printing with the influence of the church. And that style today can be embodied in modern work by means of typographic material, black text types, missal initials, and liberal use of color. But it will always be associated by the power of tradition with church literature and ecclesiastical printing.

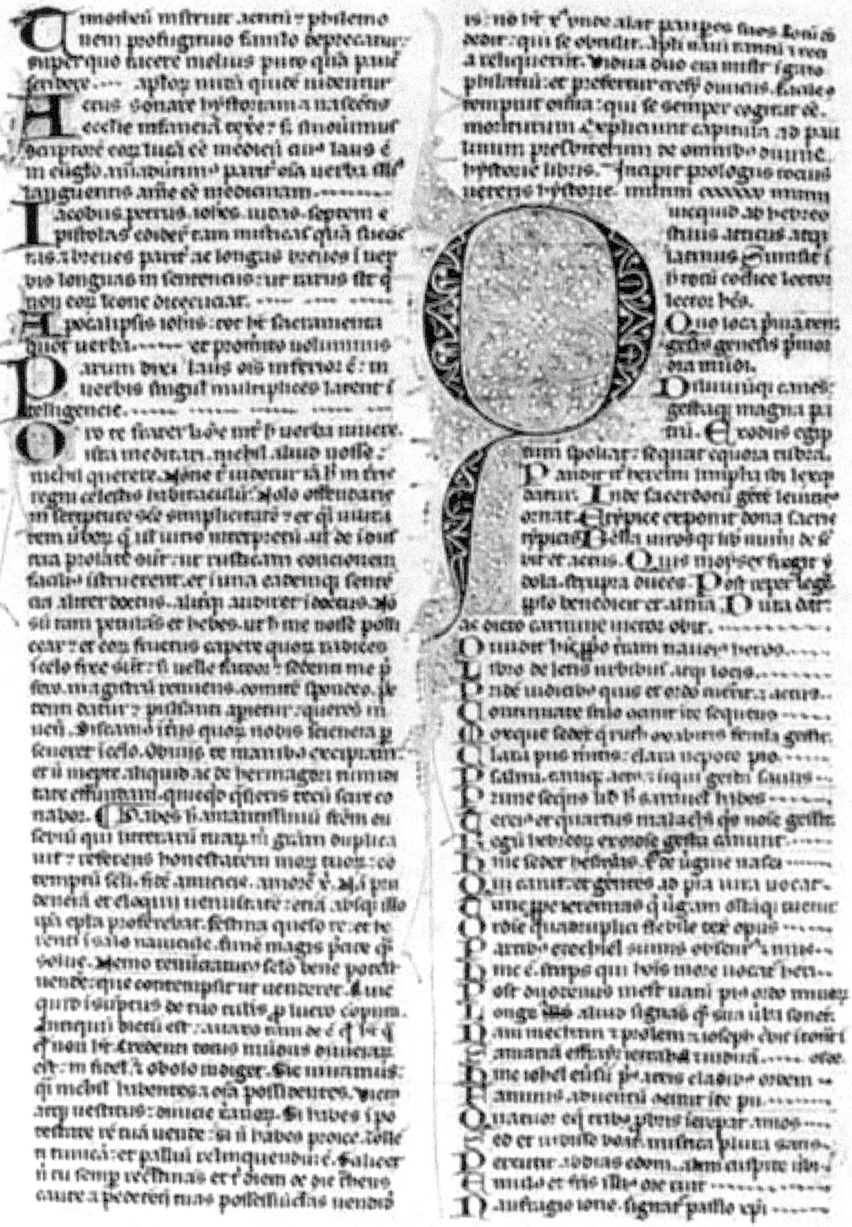

Fig. 30. A reproduction, greatly reduced, of a page from a Manuscript Bible of the early 14th Century. Entirely the product of the quill and brush of the writer and illuminator. Such books were usually done in black ink on parchment or vellum and decorated in water colors and gold leaf.

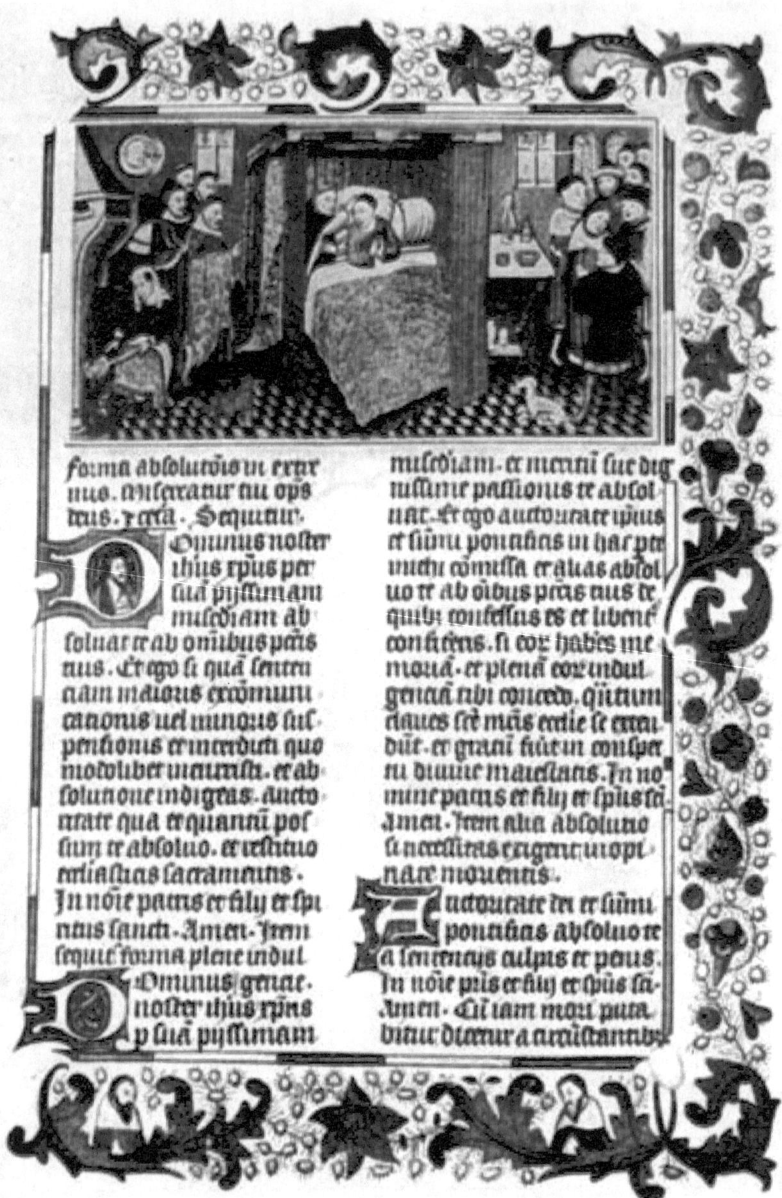

Fig. 31. A page from an illuminated Flemish manuscript of the middle 15th Century, showing characteristic treatment of illustration and decoration. This and the preceding example are shown for comparison with Figs. 32 and 33. They demonstrate the effect of the writing of books upon the development of printing.

Perhaps it was fortunate for the future of the printing art that the upheaval in Mainz drove printers out of the restricted atmosphere in which their craft was growing. For with the spread of printing into Italy, where printers sought freer fields, there straightway came a marked change in its use. The first Roman type was cut and the printers grew under the influence of the most splendid period in the history of art, the Italian Renaissance, the revival and further development of the arts which had well-nigh perished through the dark centuries. The purity of line and form, the severe dignity, and the almost too perfect proportion which had been developed by the Greeks over a thousand years before were revived and interpreted with more human feeling by the Italians of the fifteenth century.

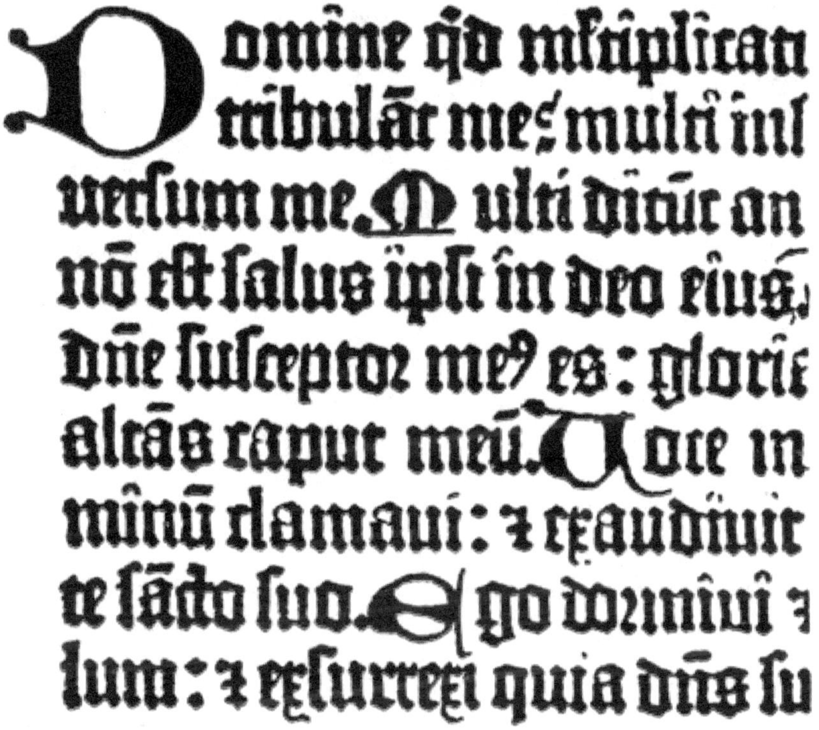

Fig. 32. Type of the Mazarin Bible (exact size).

Just as Gutenberg, Fust and Schoeffer set a standard in ecclesiastical printing with their first efforts, so Nicholas Jenson in cutting his first Roman type established a precedent which has lived to the present day.

Designers of today find inspiration in the classic expression of the Greeks for printed work which is to be similarly restrained and dignified. Type faces have been developed which are distinctly classic in feeling, echoing the letter-forms of the inscriptions which were cut in stone by Greek and Roman artisans. (Figs. 35-6.)

The design of the Renaissance has been embodied in the books of many nations. Indeed, it may be said that modern book design dates from the start of printing in Italy. But, just as the fine arts have never since flourished as they did in that resplendent period, so has the progress of design in printing been a matter of the work of individuals or limited groups rather than the character of a period or a national expression.

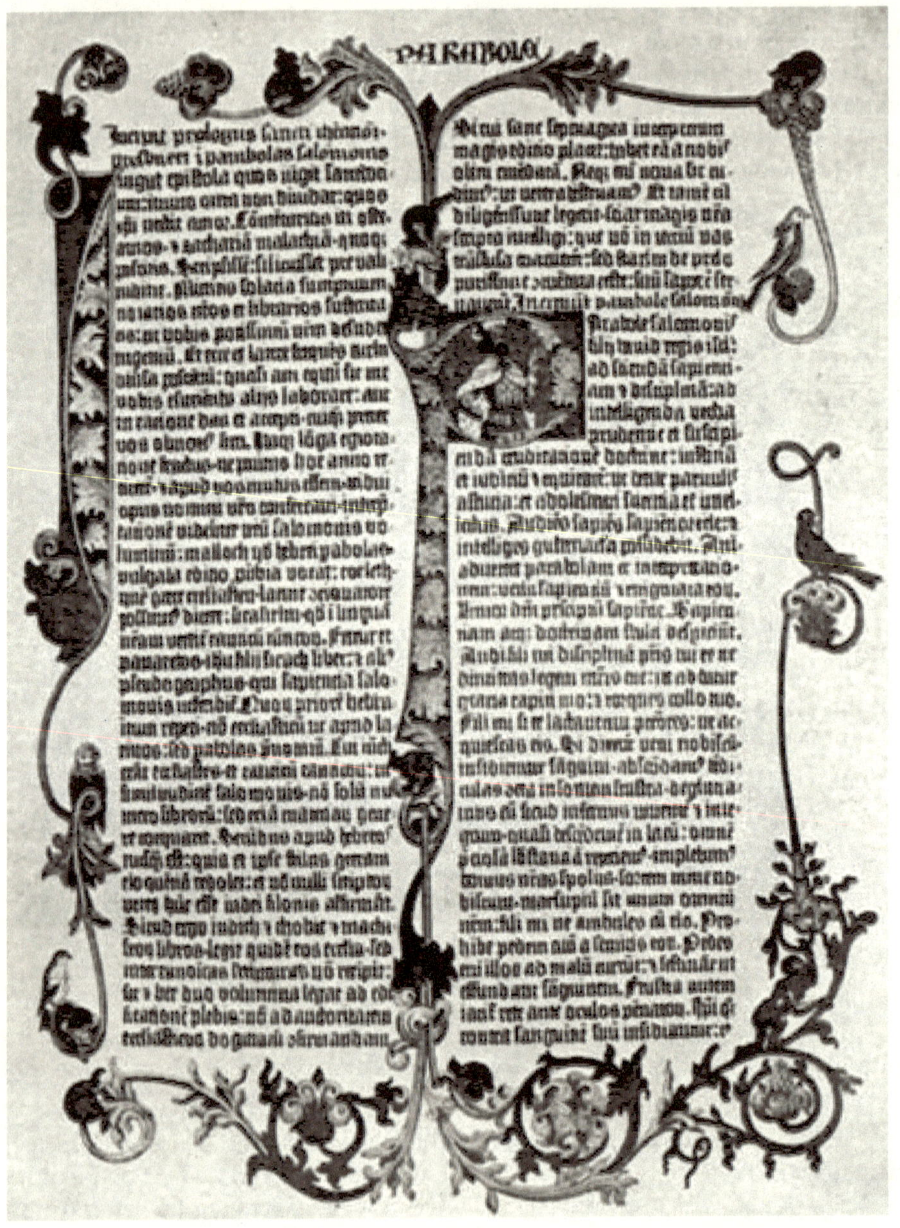

Fig. 33. Reproduction of a page from Gutenberg's 42-line Bible, of which it has been said that no later book has been more beautifully designed. In completing this book and for some years after, the illuminating and decoration were done by hand, only the type being set and printed on the press.

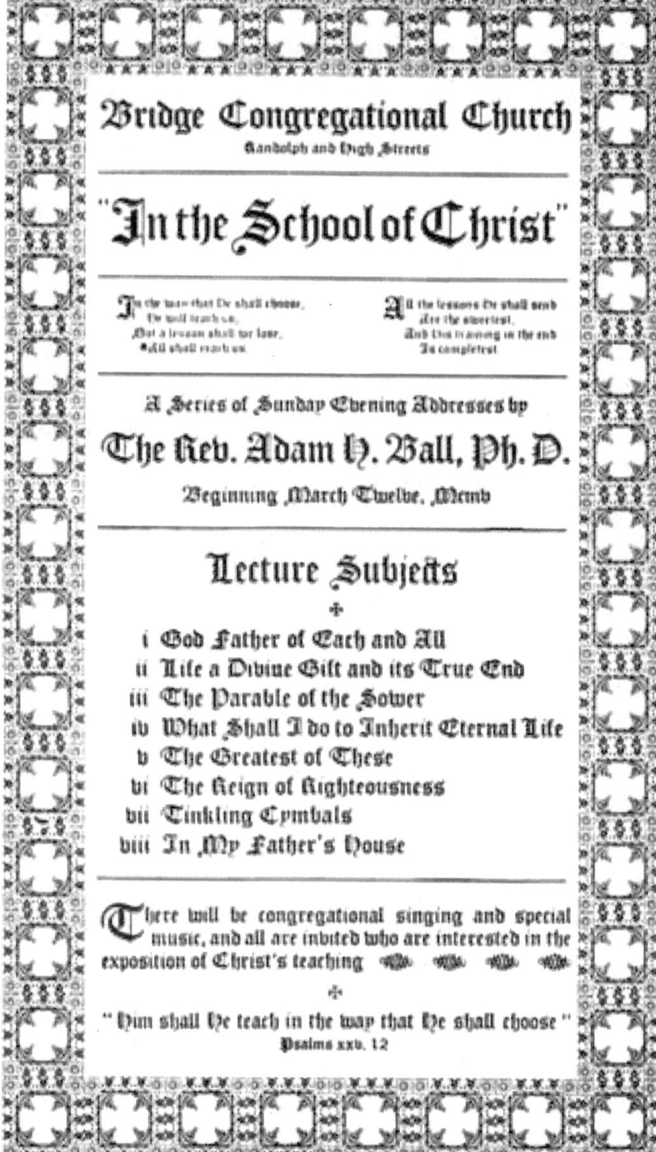

Fig. 34. Ecclesiastical style in modern typography.

The voluptuous vagaries of the successive French periods of design gave little lasting distinction to contemporary printing.

Type faces were cut at various times and by men of different nationalities which have marked characteristics, but they are not to be noted as establishing periods or styles in printing.

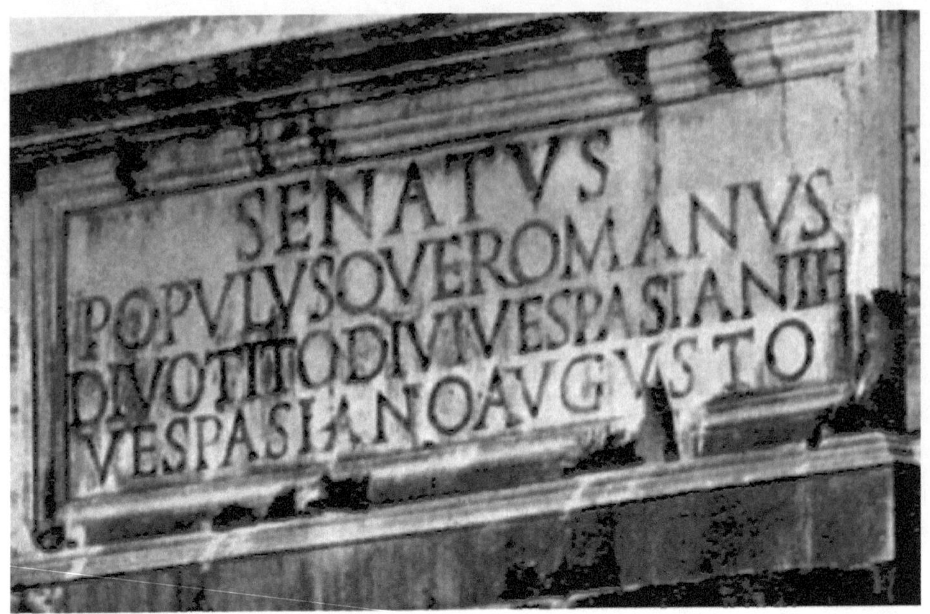

Fig. 35. An inscription in Classic Roman. Study opposite illustration.

In the seventeenth and eighteenth centuries printing in England grew into forms of expression which have been recognized under the term of "Georgian" or "colonial." The first editions of Shakespeare typify the earlier development of this style, which was marked by poor typographical materials that were nevertheless arranged in a direct and interesting manner. (Fig. 37.)

A few years later the growth of printing in the American colonies brought this form of typographic expression into most of the printed matter which has been preserved. The museums of printing and the literature dealing with the times are rich with examples. See Figs. 39 to 41.

Through the ensuing decades printing developed mechanically, but it lapsed into styles which had little or no relationship to design. It is interesting historically to follow the efforts of the printers who rode on the first steamboats and railroad trains; who recorded the rise and fall of slavery and secession; who bent their rules and jumbled their type faces during the "early Pullman days" that marked the start of many modern successful printers. The history of the craft through all these times has been picturesque and closely identified with the growth of the country. But it has little or no significance for the designer.

THE GLORY OF
THE ROMAN ALPHABET LIES IN
ITS CAPITALS WHILE THAT OF THE
GOTHIC TEXT-LETTER LIES IN ITS
LOWER CASE ⋅ THIS IS BUT NATU-
RAL AS THE ROMAN ALPHABET
ORIGINALLY WAS AN ALPHABET
OF CAPITALS ONLY

Fig. 36. Forum, a Classic Roman type, designed by Mr. F. W. Goudy.

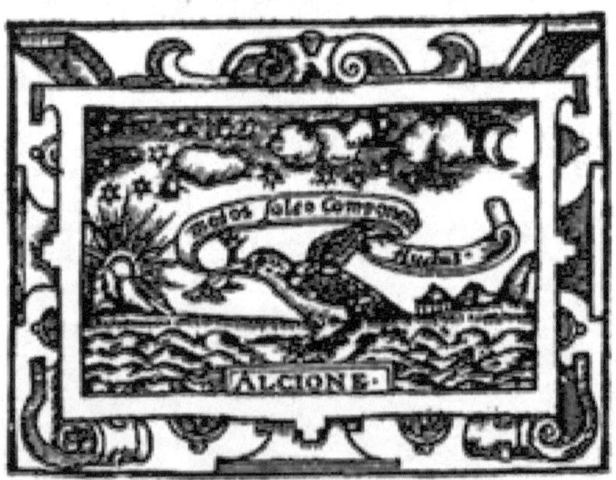

Fig. 37. Title page, much reduced, of a Shakespeare first folio, showing the Georgian style of typography. The types were poorly fitted and of uncertain alignment. The "stock" ornaments, cut on wood, were often bruised and worn. Yet there is undeniable charm in the result.

Kalendarium Pennſilvanienſe,

OR,

America's Meſſinger.

BEING AN

ALMANACK

For the Year of Grace, 1686.

Wherein is contained both the Engliſh & Forreign Account, the Motions of the Planets through the Signs, with the Luminaries, Conjunctions, Aſpects, Eclipſes; the riſing, fouthing and ſetting of the Moon, with the time when ſhe paſſeth by, or is with the moſt eminent fixed Stars : Sun riſing and ſetting and the time of High-Water at the City of *Phi-ladelphia, &c.*

With Chronologies, and many other Notes, Rules, and Tables, very fitting for every man to know & have ; all which is accomodated to the Longitude of the Province of *Pennſilvania,* and Latitude of 40 Degr. north, with a Table of Houſes for the fame, which may indifferently ſerve *New-England, New York, Eaſt & Weſt Jerſey, Maryland,* and moſt parts of *Virginia.*

By *SAMUEL ATKINS.*

Student in the Mathamaticks and Aſtrology.

And the Stars in their Courſes fought againſt Seſera, Jndg. 5. 29.

Printed and Sold by *William Bradford,* fold alſo by the Author and *H. Murrey* in *Philadelphia,* and *Philip Richards* in *New-York;* 1685.

Fig. 38. An early American page, dated 1685, showing the influence of the Georgian style upon the Colonial printers. An improvement in mechanical quality may be noted. Large capitals, a profusion of italics, and frequent use of cross rules mark this period of printing.

Design in printing has suffered through the marvelous mechanical development of machines and devices whose sole purpose has been to multiply gross output. Necessary as sheer volume of production has been, it has remained for very recent years to witness a renewal of interest in the beauty of printing, as determined by the principles of design.

William Morris, in England, devoted a very few years, toward the end of his life, to a protest against the commonplace and mechanical qualities which had dominated printing previously. He revived many of the old traditions and marked his books with his strong personality. We owe much of our present wide-spread reverence for good design in printing to his influence, even as we are similarly indebted to him for the well-designed and useful appurtenances of our daily life which have supplanted twisted and distorted furniture, stuffed birds under glass jars, and all the atrocities of a generation or two ago. See Figs.

Among the present-day designers of printing whose work shows an intimate study of the principles and the traditions of the craft are such men as Rogers, Updike, Goudy, Cleland, and Currier. The product of their work may frequently be seen in reproductions in the trade publications. It should be studied by younger designers, for it shows the results of earnest and understanding effort to make modern printing reach and even pass the artistic standards which were established nearly five hundred years ago.

Poor Richard, 1733.

A N

Almanack

For the Year of Christ

1733,

Being the First after LEAP YEAR.

And makes since the Creation	Years
By the Account of the Eastern *Greeks*	7241
By the Latin Church, when ☉ ent. ♈	6932
By the Computation of *W. W.*	5742
By the *Roman* Chronology	5682
By the *Jewish* Rabbies.	5494

Wherein is contained

The Lunations, Eclipses, Judgment of the Weather, Spring Tides, Planets Motions & mutual Aspects, Sun and Moon's Rising and Setting, Length of Days, Time of High Water, Fairs, Courts, and observable Days.

Fitted to the Latitude of Forty Degrees, and a Meridian of Five Hours West from *London*, but may without sensible Error, serve all the adjacent Places, even from *Newfoundland* to *South-Carolina.*

By *RICHARD SAUNDERS,* Philom.

PHILADELPHIA:
Printed and sold by *B. FRANKLIN,* at the New-Printing-Office near the Market

Fig. 39. Page from Poor Richard's Almanack, one of the best known of the Colonial publications. Its style is typical of that period.

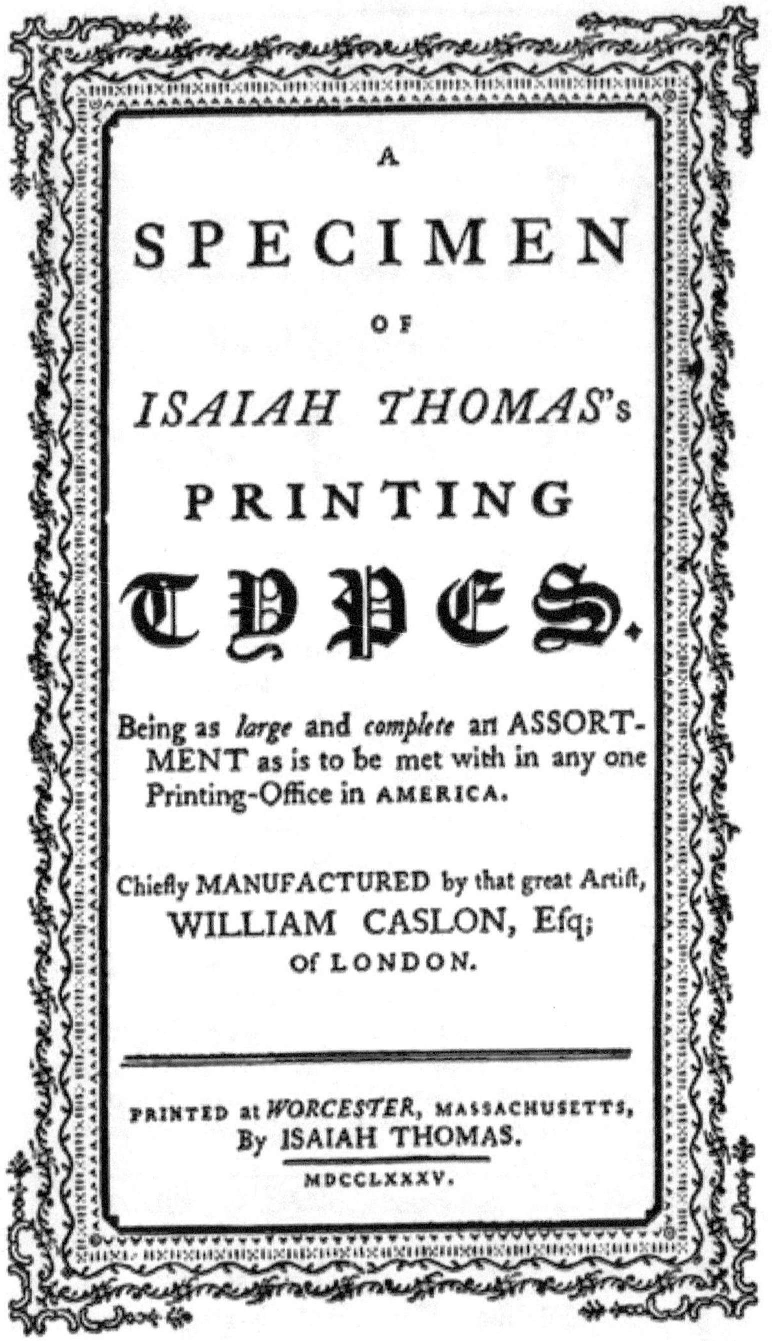

Fig. 40. Illustrating the period of transition from the true Colonial style. Type and material are obviously improved in mechanical qualities, but the compositor must have been seeking for "something new" in typography.

THE

HISTORY OF PRINTING

IN

AMERICA.

WITH A

BIOGRAPHY OF PRINTERS,

AND AN

ACCOUNT OF NEWSPAPERS.

TO WHICH IS PREFIXED A CONCISE VIEW OF

THE DISCOVERY AND PROGRESS OF THE ART

IN

OTHER PARTS OF THE WORLD.

IN TWO VOLUMES.

BY ISAIAH THOMAS

PRINTER, WORCESTER, MASSACHUSETTS.

VOLUME I.

PRINTING dispels the gloom of mental night—
Hail' pleasing fountain of all cheering light!
How like the radiant orb which gives the day,
And o'er the earth sends forth th' enlight'ning ray!

WORCESTER:

FROM THE PRESS OF ISAIAH THOMAS, JUN.
ISAAC STURTEVANT, PRINTER.

1810.

Fig. 41. Showing a typical title page composed at the beginning of the decline of typography in America. During almost the entire 19th Century there was neither reason nor design in most of the printing produced.

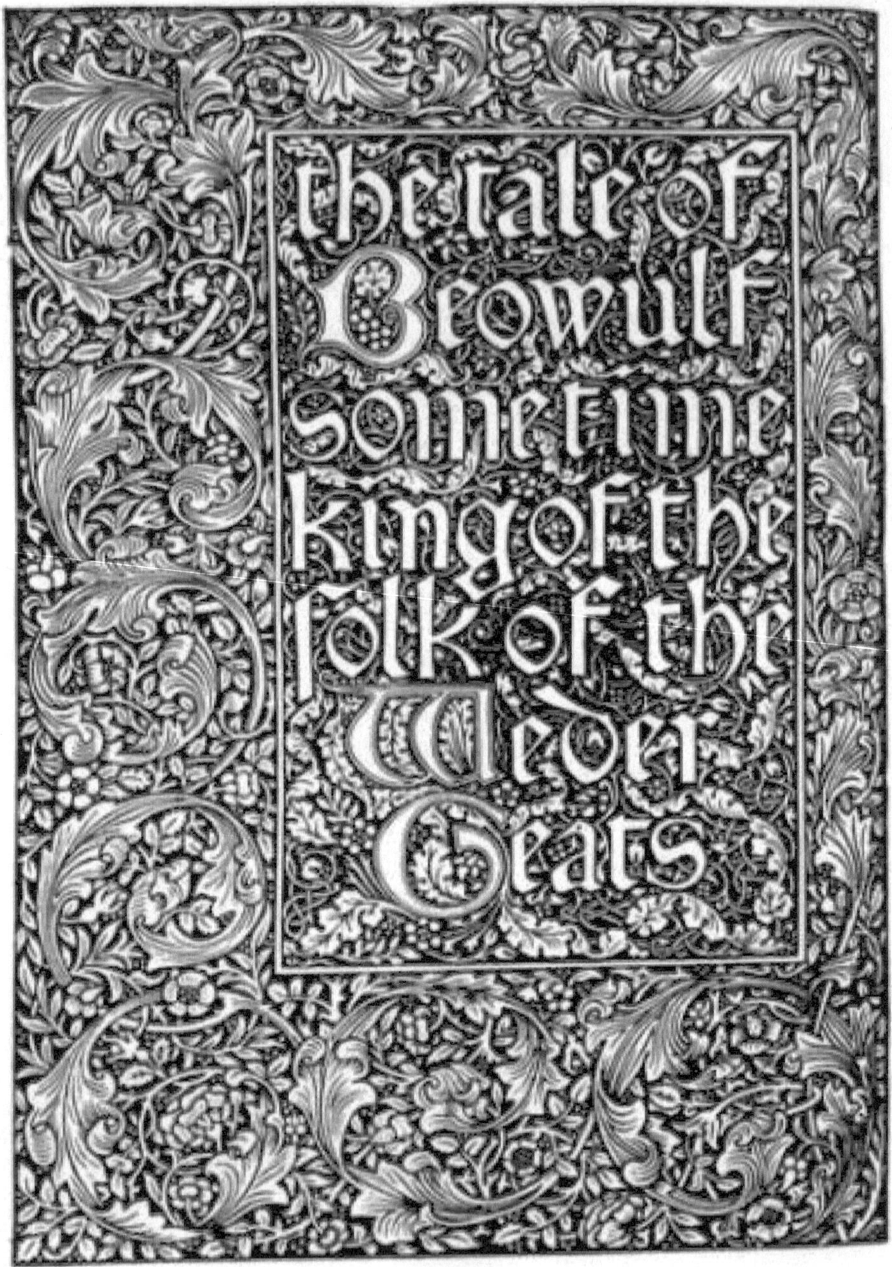

Figs. 42 and 43. Facing pages from "The Tale of Beowulf," as designed and printed by William Morris. The small reproductions give but a suggestion of the Morris conception of book-making.

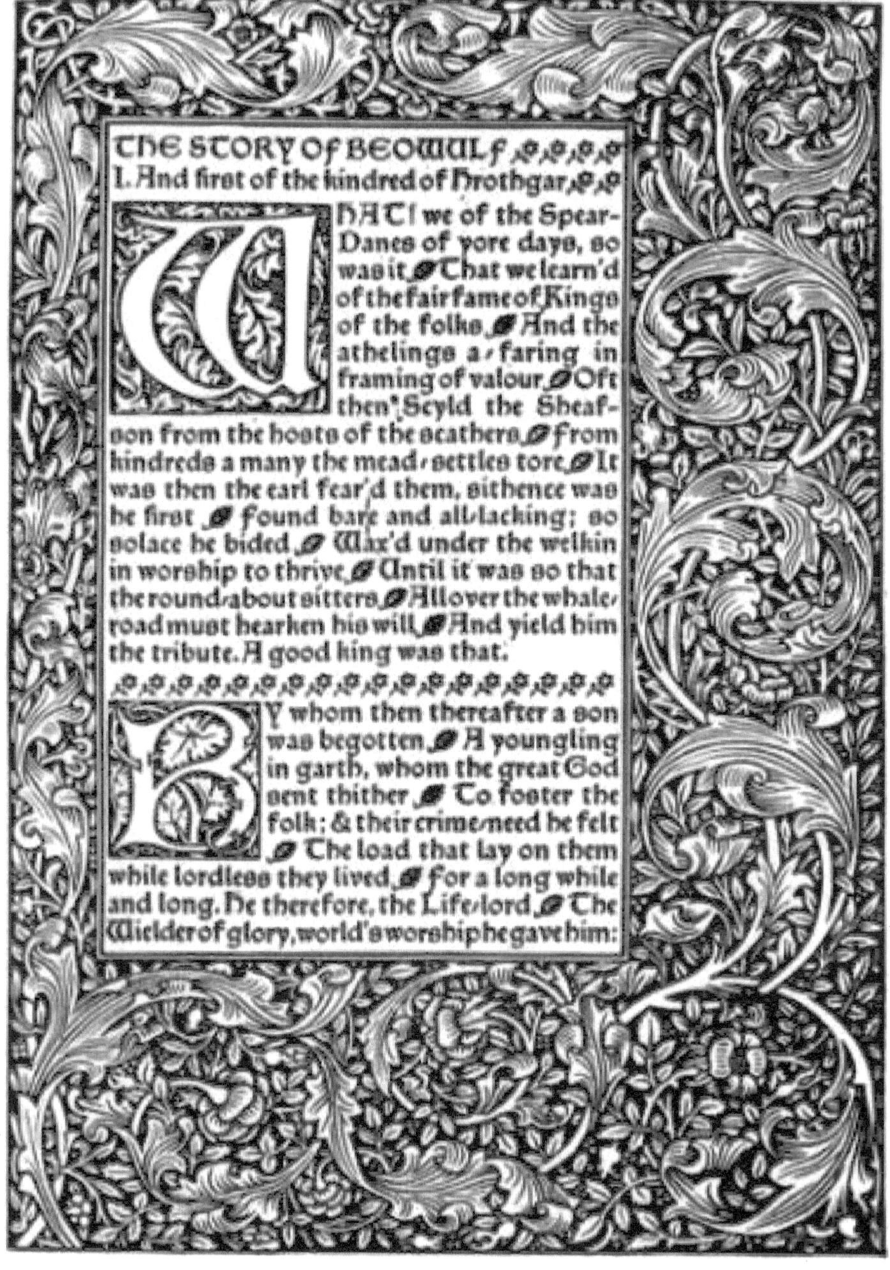

After a century or more of the most haphazard printing, Morris revived the traditions of the first book-makers, thereby stimulating a world-wide renewal of interest in typography and design.

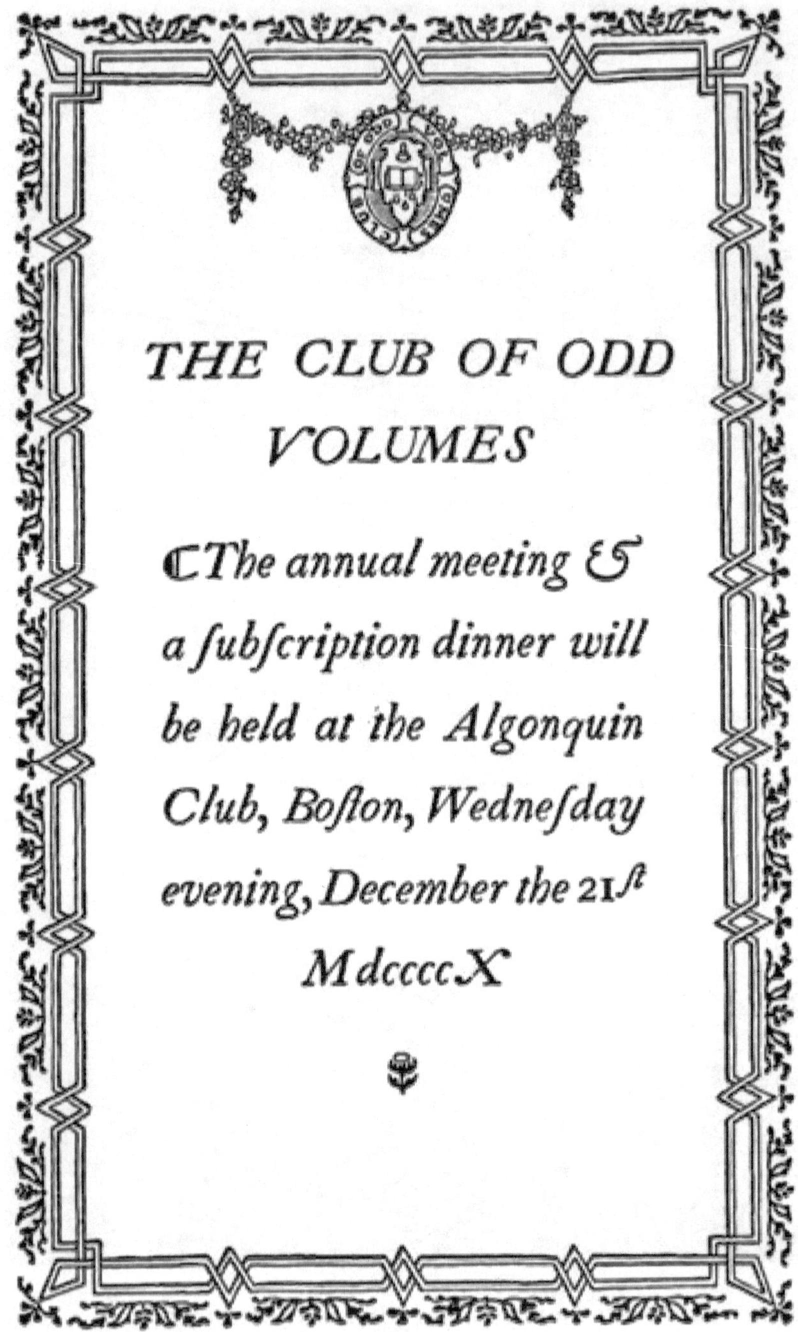

Fig. 44. Page designed by Mr. Bruce Rogers.

THE DOOR IN THE WALL

And Other Stories

BY

H·G·WELLS

ILLUSTRATED
WITH PHOTOGRAVURES FROM
PHOTOGRAPHS BY

ALVIN LANGDON COBURN

NEW YORK & LONDON
MITCHELL KENNERLEY
MCMXI

Fig. 45. Title page by Mr. F. W. Goudy.

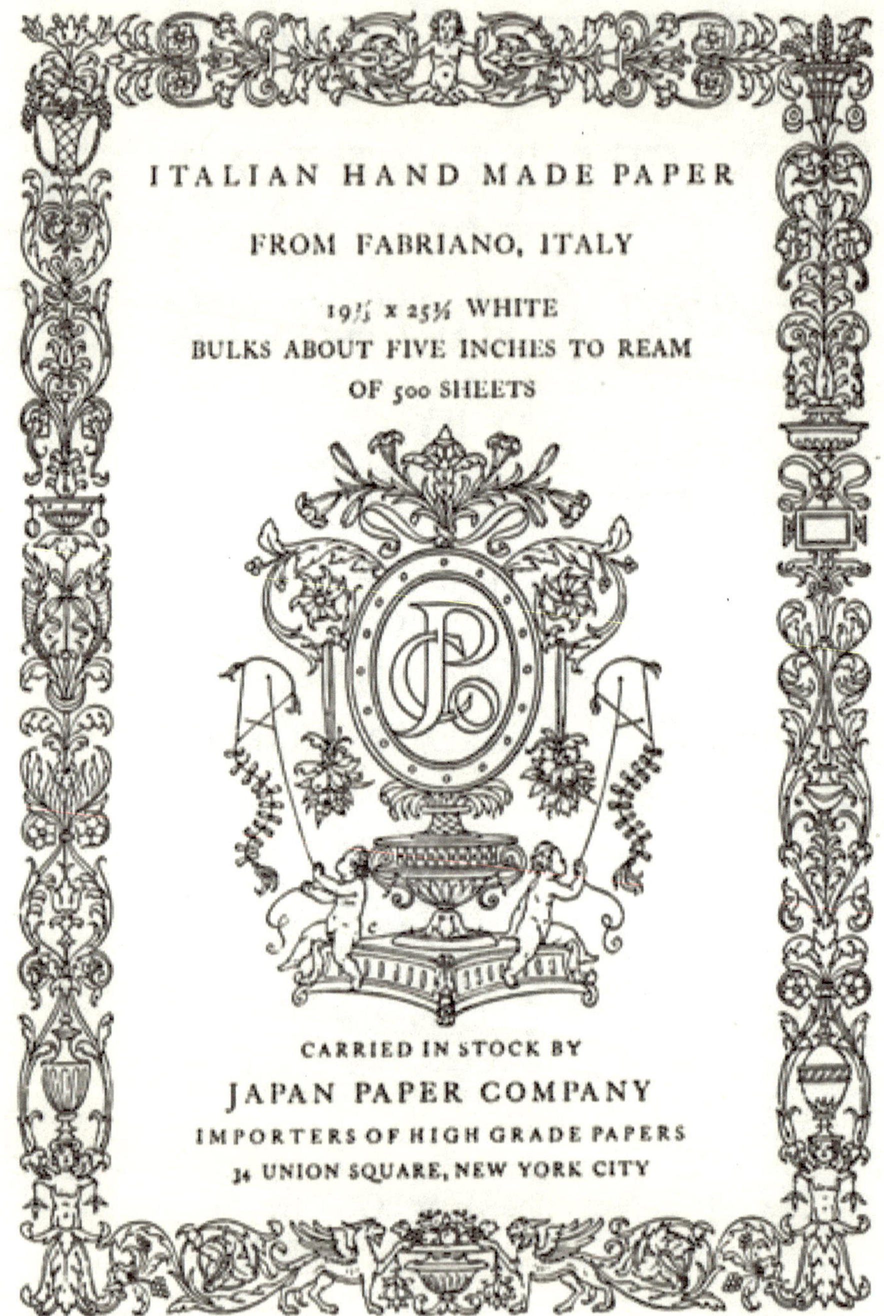

Fig. 46. Folder cover arranged by Mr. T. M. Cleleand.

MEMORIAL EXHIBITION

OF THE WORKS

OF

AUGUSTUS SAINT-GAUDENS

1

BERNARD P. E. SAINT-GAUDENS
Bronze bust, signed and dated 1867. H. 15 *in.*
Three-quarters size, directed and looking left.

Inscription
BERNARD P. E. SAINT-GAVDENS.

Signature
A. ST. G. FECIT. 1867.

Lent by Mrs. Augustus Saint-Gaudens.

NOTE. *Father of the sculptor.*

2

SILENCE
Marble statue, signed and dated 1874. *Heroic size. Female figure standing, dressed in long chiton, directed and facing to front; over the head a cloak which partially covers the face; the right hand raised, forefinger on lips, the left fore-arm raised and extended.*

Signature (in script)
AUG. S[T]. GAUDENS FECIT. ROMA 1874.

Lent by the President and Trustees of the Grand Lodge of Free and Accepted Masons of the State of New York.

Fig. 47. Catalogue page by Mr. D. B. Updike..

SUPPLEMENTARY READING

The Principles of Design. By Ernest Allen Batchelder. Inland Printer Company, Chicago.

Design in Theory and Practice. By Ernest Allen Batchelder. MacMillan Company, New York.

A Manual of Historic Ornament. By Richard Glazier. B. T. Batsford, 94 High Holburn, London.

Line and Form. By Walter Crane. G. Bell and Sons, London.

The Bases of Design. By Walter Crane. G. Bell and Sons, London.

A History of Ornament. By A. D. F. Hamlin. Century Company, New York.

Ornament and Its Application. By Lewis F. Day. Scribner's, New York.

Nature in Ornament. By Lewis F. Day. B. T. Batsford, 94 High Holburn, London.

REVIEW QUESTIONS

SUGGESTIONS TO STUDENTS AND INSTRUCTORS

The following questions, based on the contents of this pamphlet, are intended to serve (1) as a guide to the study of the text, (2) as an aid to the student in putting the information contained into definite statements without actually memorizing the text, (3) as a means of securing from the student a reproduction of the information in his own words.

A careful following of the questions by the reader will insure full acquaintance with every part of the text, avoiding the accidental omission of what might be of value. These primers are so condensed that nothing should be omitted.

In teaching from these books it is very important that these questions and such others as may occur to the teacher should be made the basis of frequent written work, and of final examinations.

The importance of written work cannot be overstated. It not only assures knowledge of material but the power to express that knowledge correctly and in good form.

QUESTIONS

1. What purpose in the works of mankind is served by design?

2. In what manner does design influence man's handiwork?

3. What is design?

4. What is "a design"?

5. What is the difference between beauty and fitness to purpose?

6. What are the elements of design?

7. What relationship has a printer to a sculptor, an architect, a painter, a decorative designer?

8. How does the printed page limit its design?

9. What is the difference between a printed picture and a printed design based upon that picture?

10. Why are pictures unsuitable to decorate a printed page? .

11. What are the materials of design?

12. Analyze a well-designed typographical ornament into the materials which

compose it.

13. When the materials of design are put to use, what conditions must be satisfied in their arrangement?

14. What is harmony?

15. What is balance?

16. What is proportion?

17. What is rhythm?

18. How may the foregoing qualities be demonstrated?

19. What shapes should be used in combination?

20. What further relationship should they have?

21. On a type page 20 picas wide by 30 picas deep would a panel 18 picas wide by 8 picas deep be proper? What, if anything, would be preferable?

22. Would a rule line 6 points wide be suitable to surround a mass of 18 point Caslon old style caps? Why?

23. If the printed page is to be other than black and white, what further consideration of harmony is involved?

24. What must we consider in related areas with respect to their size or measure?

25. What relationship of sizes is often most interesting?

26. Place a single line on a cover page in a desirable position.

27. Is the eye always to be trusted in the judgment of space relationships?

28. Should mathematical measurements or the effect upon the eye be the guiding factor in arrangement? Why?

29. What is the effect of the surrounding edge or border upon the masses of a design?

30. How should the masses in a design be arranged with respect to the surrounding edge?

31. What mathematical principles influence this arrangement?

32. How is equality in the halves of a printed page sometimes desirable and sometimes not?

33. When there is no equality in the halves of a design, what condition exists and what principles must guide such an arrangement?

34. What is ornament?

35. What qualities may ornament possess? Define them.

36. In what periods of design does each quality appear most pronouncedly?

37. How is ornament related to nature? To inventiveness or ingenuity?

38. How is ornament related to mathematics?

39. What are the important divisions of mathematical ornament?

40. What happens when an ornament is developed from a natural source?

41. What is the source called?

42. What periods of design have most affected printing? Why?

43. Explain how each of the above periods influences modern typography.

44. What should be the typographer's attitude toward the activities of designers of every age and period?

45. What has been the effect of mechanical development in printing upon typographic design?

46. Name some of the modern men whose work is of interest to the typographer.

GLOSSARY
TERMS OF DESIGN AS APPLIED TO PRINTING

Assyrian (Art)—The Assyrian Empire lay in Southwestern Asia between the Tigris and the Euphrates, now part of Turkey in Asia. Its art was largely expressed in the treatment of flat surfaces, using enameled bricks, painted stuccoes, figured bronzes, etc. Bricks were the only building material. The period dates from 4000-3000 B.C. to about 500 B.C.

Attraction—The force exercised upon the eye by a mass through its tone, color, size, or shape.

Axis—A line dividing a surface for purpose of comparison or construction.

Balance—An apparent state of rest between the various attractions in a design. To balance the elements of a design is to arrange them so that they are set at rest with one another.

Byzantine (Art)—The art of Eastern Christendom, from the time when Byzantium (now Constantinople) became the capital in 330 A.D. until the taking of the city by the Turks in 1453 and even later. Byzantine art embodied Asiatic luxury in splendor and in profusion of color and gilding. Its forms of design were purely geometrical and conventional, with no use of the human figure.

Celtic (Art)—Particularly active in the fourth century among the people of what are now the British Isles. It was influenced by Central Asia and Persia, and is thus somewhat oriental.

Chinese (Art)—Characterized by the use of fantastic forms and brilliant color. Best exemplified in porcelains, lacquers, and carvings in wood and semi-precious stones. The source of inspiration of the Japanese who have commercialized and cheapened it in everything save wood-block cutting and printing.

Classic—The period of early Greece and Rome.

Colonial (Art)—Found in the printing and other applied design of the early American colonies and during the first years of the American Republic. Derived from England and sometimes called "Georgian."

Color—The kind of light reflected by a surface.

Conception—The process of forming an idea or scheme.

DECORATION—Any thing or group of things that embellishes or adorns.

DESIGN (In general)—An arrangement of forms or colors, or both, intended to be executed in hard substances or pliable material or to be applied to a fabric or other surface for ornament. (In printing)—The arrangement of masses, lines, and dots to secure the qualities of beauty, and fitness. (Specific)—"A design": any piece of work into which the elements of design have been incorporated.

EGYPTIAN (Art)—Includes the period of art activity in Egypt dating from about 4000 B.C. through successive steps to 500 B.C. It was highly conventionalized, richly decorated, making use of material forms interpreted with vigorous color. In architecture its chief characteristic was durability.

ESTHETIC—Pertaining to beauty as manifested in the fine arts. "The esthetic imagination differs from the scientific.... The difference is seen in the fact that the end is no longer knowledge but beauty."

ECCLESIASTICAL (Style)—That which characterized the books and manuscripts of the early churches, usually in black text letter forms with elaborate ornamentation and illumination.

GEOMETRICAL (Design)—Based upon spots, bands, or all-over patterns made up of straight and curved lines developed geometrically.

GEORGIAN (Period)—Included the English and Colonial American design of the 17th and 18th centuries. Similar to "Colonial."

GOTHIC (Art)—Developed in the architecture and applied design in Europe from 1200 A.D. to 1500 A.D. Characterized by vertical lines, pointed arches, and decorative material based directly upon nature.

GREEK (Design)—That of early Greece, dated from about 620 B.C. to about 350 B.C., developed under the influence of Egypt and Assyria but rising far above either in purity and expression. "The Greek artisan had the unerring taste of the artist and sought his inspiration from the same sources."

HARMONY (In art)—A state of completeness in the relationship to things to each other.

HEADBAND—The horizontal strip of decoration used to ornament or to set off a type page.

INDIAN (Art)—That of the East Indies or India, which have several styles, all oriental in character. American Indian art was manifested in geometric ornament, raw colors, and crude representation of animate forms.

INITIAL LETTER—A large letter, unornamented or decoratively designed, used to mark the beginning of a chapter, an important change in the text, or to decorate a single mass of type.

JAPANESE (Design)—Derived from the Chinese and usually commercialized in its application. Of chief interest to printers in the arrangement and rendering of wood-block prints.

MAHOMETANS—Followers of the Prophet Mahomet, including Arabian, Indian, Moorish, Persian, and other nations.

MASS—One of the main portions of a design, readily distinguished and having some unity in itself, yet remaining in proper relationship to the whole scheme.

MATERIALS OF DESIGN—Masses, dots, and lines which compose the completed design.

MOTIF—The original source for a decorative scheme or element.

NATURAL FORMS—Motifs of design chosen from nature, either animate or inanimate.

NATURALISTIC (Design)—The direct imitation of forms taken from nature, retaining as much as possible of their original shape, color, etc.

OPTICAL ILLUSION—An error, normal to the average eye, in the perception of certain lines, angles, and spaces. Recognized by the designers of type and of typography.

ORNAMENT—Similar to decoration.

PERSIAN (Art)—Covered by the period from about 550 B.C. to 330 B.C. Derived from Assyrian art but strongly influenced by the Greek.

POINT OF BALANCE—The point, unindicated in the finished design, upon which the various attractions of the design are balanced in appearance.

PROPORTION—The comparative relationship between the various elements in a design.

RENAISSANCE—The period of art activity in the 14th and 15th centuriesin Italy. A revival of the classic arts but developed and enriched beyond former heights.

RHYTHM—Movement, characterized by the regular recurrence of accent or motion.

ROMAN (Design)—A transplanted development of Greek design, influenced by Roman habits and character. More realistic in the treatment of natural forms than the Greek.

SHAPE—The contour or appearance of an area.

SCANDINAVIAN (Design)—That of the nations Denmark, Norway, and Sweden, characterized by rich interlacements, and many symbolic devices.

SYMBOLIC—Typifying or representing the idea or purpose of a design.

SYMMETRY—Regular arrangement of parts across a given axis, so that a division through that axis will give similar halves.

TONE—The amount (not kind) of light reflected from a given surface—"a light tone" or "dark in tone."

VARIETY—An intermixture of elements in a design different in form or color and not arranged symmetrically.

Lector House believes that a society develops through a two-fold approach of continuous learning and adaptation, which is derived from the study of classic literary works spread across the historic timeline of literature records. Therefore, we aim at reviving, repairing and redeveloping all those inaccessible or damaged but historically as well as culturally important literature across subjects so that the future generations may have an opportunity to study and learn from past works to embark upon a journey of creating a better future.

This book is a result of an effort made by Lector House towards making a contribution to the preservation and repair of original ancient works which might hold historical significance to the approach of continuous learning across subjects.

HAPPY READING & LEARNING!

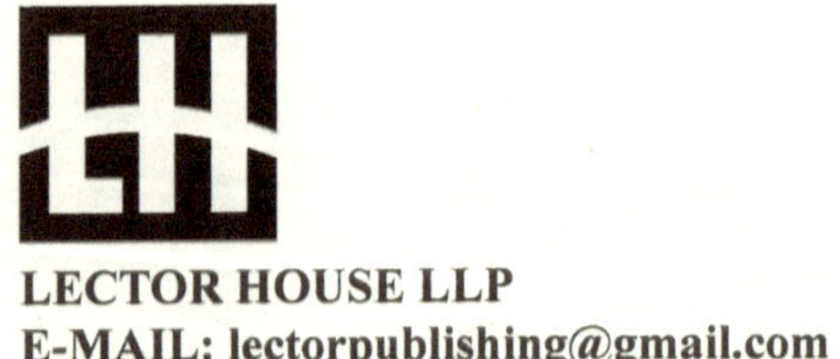

LECTOR HOUSE LLP
E-MAIL: lectorpublishing@gmail.com

9 789354 201790